edition taberna kritika

Die edition taberna kritika wird vom Bundesamt für Kultur (CH) mit einem Förderbeitrag für die Jahre 2021–2024 unterstützt.

Shelby Stuart
Schwyz.Uri.Unterwalden.

http://www.etkbooks.com/
Gestaltung: etkbooks, Bern
Coverillustration: Shelby Stuart

Bibliografische Information der Deutschen Nationalbibliothek:
Die Deutsche Nationalbibliothek verzeichnet diese Publikation in der Deutschen Nationalbibliografie; detaillierte bibliografische Daten sind im Internet über http://www.dnb.de abrufbar.

ISBN: 978-3-905846-73-7

Shelby Stuart

Schwyz.Uri.Unterwalden.

Zweisprachige Ausgabe

Translated from the English
by Beatrice Minger

Mit einem Nachwort
von Christian de Simoni

edition taberna kritika

INTRODUCTION

„Before I had studied Zen for thirty years, I saw mountains as mountains, and rivers as rivers. When I arrived at a more intimate knowledge, I came to the point where I saw that mountains are not mountains, and rivers are not rivers. But now that I have got its very substance I am at rest. For it's just that I see mountains once again as mountains, and rivers once again as rivers.“

Ch'ing-yüan Wei-hsin

Before I ever had a role in the story – before a visa, a job, a circle of friends, an apartment – before I ever had a Swiss love interest to validate my presence in this country, I was often asked:

Why are you here?

Why Switzerland?

I never knew how to justify what felt like coming home.

My great-grandfather was Swiss, but he had long ago given up his place here. However much I romanticized his history as a way to claim my roots, I also had ancestors from France, Germany, England and beyond. There was no clear lineage of belonging.

I once came across an Article of Naturalization in Swiss law entitled, „Erroneous assumption of Swiss Citizenship".

It states:

A foreign national who for at least five years has believed in good faith that he or she is a Swiss citizen and during this period has actually been treated as such by the cantonal or communal authorities may be naturalized under the simplified procedure.

At first, I laughed, almost hopefully, at the absurdity of a law based on belief. Although my research confirmed that the article was rarely put into practice, it was an idea that seemed fitting to the roots of the Reformation in the country. Denying the Pope´s authority as the mediator of redemption, the religious movement preached the power of faith over good works.

If one could gain salvation by faith, why not nationality? What if, when asked why I am here, I simply answer: I believe.

The etymology of the verb *belong*, dating back to the late 14th century, was used to connote ownership: „to be the property of" or „to be a member of". The definition implies that to belong is only possible once the terms of possession have been set, and the lines of affiliation clearly drawn.

What is fixed is functional. When the boundaries stay in place, so do we. We belong.

My first morning in the country, I woke up late in the home of a distant relative. The cool air drifted through the open window and before I had even opened my eyes, I could smell the damp earth and the freshness of the grass after the rain.

I had stirred only once during the night when from beneath the warmth of my feather duvet, I had heard the gentle drumming against the rooftop.

My host had woken up much earlier, so I came down the wooden steps into an empty kitchen where an iron pot of tea was waiting, kept warm by the heat of a candle. Beside it, a loaf of bread sat on a cutting board full of cheeses, firm tangy blocks and sweet rounds of white that cut softer than butter.

I could hear thunder beginning to rumble over the Alps in the distance. Across the valley, the peaks were half-buried in clouds, but I could still make out traces of their powerful figures framing the view.

At the time, I was a month shy of 21. Initially intending to stay in Europe for only three months, I postponed my university studies and prolonged my stay in Switzerland to a year and half, coming in and out of the country on tourist visas and panicking, with a kind of preemptive and unaccountable longing, each time I had to leave.

My body, oblivious to immigration laws, had seemed to settle into place. My shoulders dropped, my breath deepened, my weight sank into the soil as if for the first time I had found ground beneath my feet. In a land where I was a foreigner, I felt an irrational impulse to take root.

I had no excuse to cling to this country with family, friends and a comfortable life waiting for me in the States, but having experienced the exhalation of landing, I resisted anything that would pull me away. Young and home hungry, I was ready to follow whatever protocol was necessary, willing to undergo whatever rites of initiation would be required.

It took years to discover there were none; the answer to whether I could belong to Switzerland was simple: I could not.

I had grown up in the United States under the myth that anyone who came to the country, worked hard, and lived the American dream was one of us. Becoming American depended on one´s capacity for success against all odds – against institutionalized racism, poverty, physical pain – each obstacle overcome through sheer grit, a success the nation itself would take credit for.

Whether an immigrant was welcomed or repeatedly wronged, it was essential they hold to the belief that anything was possible, a trial by fire survived only by those worthy of coming home to the greatest country on earth.

In the 1920s, my great-grandfather had followed the script.

Approximately 90,000 Swiss citizens migrated to the United States between 1890 and 1930. My 17-year-old great-grandfather, along with his brothers, was among them. Land was cheap, industrialized agriculture was growing, and at a time of widespread xenophobia, there were advantages to being a white European male.

Having gone to America in search of work, my great-grandfather started with field labor, but slowly advanced his career as a practical engineer and eventually became an international representative for Caterpillar tractors.

Nearly a century later, Switzerland wasn´t particularly interested in the strength of my resolve to stay; there was little taste for dramatic narratives of climbing the ladder or living the dream. The immigration office assured me I was not unique. In the United States, I was one among hundreds of thousands of citizens with Swiss roots.

In the case of my belonging, the verdict was clear: I was American because my great-grandfather had made the foolish mistake of leaving home.

When I finally returned to the States to finish university, I lived in a kind of far-fetched emotional exile from an adopted homeland that would not have me. I was studying creative writing and wrote long elegiac narratives about my ancestors and all the possible reasons I might belong in Switzerland. Despite the sympathetic nods of my classmates, my arguments were inconclusive. Finally, I retreated to the local library where I borrowed stacks of outdated books on the history of Switzerland as if learning about the country´s roots might teach me how to graft my own.

As the story goes, the Swiss Confederation was founded in 1291 when Schwyz, Uri and Unterwalden, three neighboring forest cantons, each governed by the local elite, formed an alliance against the Habsburg overlords who were closing in on the region near the Gotthard.

A pledge is said to have taken place at the beginning of August on the slopes of Seelisberg leading down to Lake Lucerne where three men, representatives from each of the cantons, came together and swore an oath to protect their freedom. Similar treaties had been made between cantons before this time, but the Federal Charter of 1291 was one of the oldest to be written and preserved.

As was a common practice, the text was likely constructed through a patchwork of other agreements and then merged into a charter of its own. There are spelling mistakes and inconsistencies throughout the document, such as a shifting of pronouns that slip between „we“ and „they“. Additionally, the text is not signed and has no mention of who was present or the specific place where the pact was made.

The manuscript was lost among Schwyz archives until 1758, and even now the authenticity of its age is questioned. It wasn´t until the end of the 19th century that the government chose the formerly insignificant document to be the constitutional birth certificate of the country.

Due to the rise of political pressures in the 1930s, the Swiss Confederation struggled to form a cohesive identity, a public front with which to face the changing world. At this time, special attention was given to the Federal Charter as a symbol of freedom and independence. At the center of the country´s narrative of unity was the tale of three cantons´ bold defiance against foreign powers.

Long after the legendary oath of mutual alliance was made in 1291, Unterwalden divided into the two half cantons of Obwalden and Nidwalden. Twenty other cantons and four half cantons eventually joined the confederation to make up what we now know as modern-day Switzerland.

Fact or fiction, Schwyz, Uri and Unterwalden have become historically representative of the core of the country: this is where the roots have been drawn.

Throughout my twenties and early thirties, while finishing college and traveling between artist residencies, Switzerland remained my fixed destination. I visited as frequently as possible and planned to move back at the first opportunity.

Friends and family sometimes questioned my preoccupation with mild concern. Was it perhaps nostalgia? A state of mind I was after? What was I projecting onto the country? Did I simply want what I could not have?

I could not help but wonder the same.

My inability to articulate the ground of my obsession to others, much less to myself, didn´t help my case. When asked what it was about Switzerland that drew me and why I needed to return, I winced at my own descriptions of the country. My words sounded as if they were taken straight out of the pages of *Heidi*, a sentimental tale of an orphan girl who finds a new life in the Swiss mountains with her grandfather. She spends her days running through fields of edelweiss with goats trailing behind her. Mid-story, she is taken away to the city where she becomes so ill with homesickness, the doctor realizes the only remedy is for her to return to the Alps.

Despite my estrangement from the country, I was in good health and had no grandfather waiting for me, so there were times when even I tried to dissuade myself from the delusion of a life in Switzerland.

While living in Seattle with a good friend in a slightly dilapidated but charming house in a neighborhood we loved, I decided it was time to put aside my youthful whims and settle into the beauty of our makeshift home. I would follow others´ advice, stop wishing myself elsewhere and start appreciating my close community in a wonderful city full of possibilities.

The day after I had given myself this pep talk, my roommate came into the kitchen to tell me we had been evicted; the house would be torn down. A wave of relief washed through me. I immediately began to make plans for what I hoped would be, right or wrong, my final move to Europe.

Following a year of saving and sleeping on friends´ couches once the house was gone, I flew to Switzerland, where I spent the next two and a half years piecing together visas to keep me in the country or at least on the continent, until I finally secured my place in a master´s program in Zurich. Having exhausted the elegiac essay, I was determined to find a new form within which I could write myself into the narrative of this country.

I was a writer, my medium was the word, but for years I had been searching for a way to better understand the corporeal reality of language. Often having envied the physicality of other disciplines, I watched artists move, build, paint and sculpt their objects while I sat at a computer and typed ideas.

Intellectually I knew it was impossible to write an immaterial thought or emotion. As the philosopher John Dewey wrote, there is no such thing as fear or love, but only the specific circumstances which evoke it. Every feeling has its roots firmly planted in the physical particularity of a moment – the physical particularity of a place.

When I first arrived in Switzerland, my body had settled into the soil long before my brain could think of a good theory why. How then to write the feeling of this country? What were the sensory details of my initial attachment? Certainly, it was more than blocks of cheese and a hot cup of tea on a stormy morning, but it also was not less than that.

Isn´t a place a compilation of objects we can touch, smell and taste?

I had not initially imagined Schwyz, Uri and Unterwalden as a path to my inclusion. The names had been forgotten among the history books long since returned to the local Seattle library. Now back in Switzerland, I checked out stacks of maps in place of books, planning hikes and studying grid lines as a way to better orient myself in the country.

It was early spring and the trails were just beginning to thaw beneath the melting snow when I decided to hike a path aptly called the Alpine Panorama Trail. The bench at every vantage point seemed timed to the tourists´ gasps of wonder as a sea of Alps stretched as far as the eye could see. I briefly shared the admiration of the others on the trail but was distracted by trying to keep ahead of the crowds and eventually took a wrong turn. At last alone with the scenery, I became increasingly lost, cutting through fields of tall grass in an effort to find my way down the mountain.

Even now, I doubt I could retrace the misstep of that day on a map, but in the end, I found myself on the floor of a valley where the mountains were no longer a panoramic backdrop but an encompassing presence all around me. The predictable beauty that had felt almost trite along the trail swallowed me whole.

I don´t know what constitutes the palpability of a place, why one valley pulses with existence while another lies flat, but I had inadvertently crossed over a border and entered into a landscape I could no longer ignore.

It was only later, unfolding the map on the train ride home, that I realized I had wandered into the canton of Schwyz. Having intended to hike from Unterägeri to Zug, I had instead come down the wrong side of the mountain, following the border of Lake Ägerisee into a valley near Sattel. It was here that Schwyz had taken hold.

What fallacy was I falling for when I unconsciously stepped over the boundary of a canton and felt I was somewhere new? This was hardly the first time I had become enamored with a specific region of Switzerland, but I was compelled to understand the strength of my impression, whether it was simply the glow of the late afternoon sunlight on the valley walls, or having found my way down the mountain, the relief of walking on level ground. Profound or trivial, I wanted to probe my experience of place, an investigation which might help me better understand my own unfounded attachment to a foreign land.

After all, when people asked me, why are you here, I wanted to know too. If Switzerland was nothing more than a configuration of man-made borders, what was the draw that kept me here, circling a mere conjecture of a country I could never join?

Schwyz, along with Uri and Unterwalden, if not the true heart of Switzerland, remained symbolic of where the boundaries had first been set, and it was here I would choose to tread a path into the very concept of a country that kept me out.

Over the next nine months, I made 21 walking trips, seven through each of the founding cantons. It was a founding I knew was a myth, but one in which I was more than ready to suspend my disbelief in order to belong.

Without knowing the form the text would take, I began writing down seemingly insignificant happenings along each trail: a snake slithering across the path, the pulse of my heartbeat or a scent of wild chamomile in the still air. I wanted my words to practice the immediacy my body knew so well. As if for the first time, I experienced the inherent embodiment of language; I wrote no further than my feet could walk.

I remember taking the train from Basel to Schwyz the fourth, the fifth, the sixth time. Along the recurring route there was a thrill in recognizing the curve of the tracks, a field of hay or the profile of a mountain, but the more often I went, the more the landscape grew, making several hikes through the single canton´s 907 km^2 feel like an insignificant attempt at orientation.

How many walks would be necessary to say I knew the place? How many landmarks would I need to identify? How many villages would I need to name? The further I followed my questions, the more absurd they became.

I continued.

Every feature, every detail I discovered became a treasured familiarity. A stretch of land which had been nothing more than empty space on a map became tangible experience. I relished every imprint, from the sharp rocks pressing into the rubber sole of my shoe to my aching knees and sunburned skin, which bore witness to the encounter for days after I returned home.

In this microcosm of Switzerland, I subverted the customary pathways to belonging which I knew I could never take. I followed my projections to their logical end. I came close, so close the relationship could no longer be denied.

It was an unabashed attempt at appropriation through intimacy.

In choosing to hike through the cantons, I was intentionally following a neurosis of belonging in order to see where it might lead. Was there any end to the path of trying to usurp an entire country?

A neurosis, as defined by the *Lexico* dictionary, is: „a relatively mild mental illness that is not caused by organic disease, involving symptoms of stress (depression, anxiety, obsessive behaviour...) but not a radical loss of touch with reality".

My obsessive behavior of accumulating ground in each canton, driven by my anxiety to belong, was in fact an effort toward a radical touch with reality.

Step by step, I wove myself into the trails, attempting to bring my awareness to the minute elements of experience I might otherwise ignore. I often scanned my body to feel the wind on my neck or the weight of my feet as they shambled through dead leaves.

My question was not what is Schwyz, or Uri or Unterwalden, but what were the qualities of the places that had given rise to these names?

The answer I was after could not be found through local conversation, broad social analysis or even historical background. I was seeking something more primary, a pre-narrative relationship to the land. For this reason, I often followed trails in place of roads and found myself more often walking through fields of cows than crowds of people.

The goal was no longer to achieve objective knowledge of the region, the fullness of which I knew I could never reach, but rather to trace the sinews of connection which bound me there from one moment to the next. What was the nature of the relationship when the focus was taste, touch, smell – sensation, rather than story?

It was part of the neurosis to *almost* believe that every border of a canton or country represented a fixed reality which could alienate or include me. Mountains are mountains, rivers are rivers, but each step took me farther away from the finitude of form.

Dating back even earlier in the 14th century, long before the word was used to connote property or possession, the initial meaning of *belong* was „to properly relate to“. The intensive prefix *be-* has a variety of meanings in Old English, including „about, around, on all sides“.

To properly relate to

Belonging as relationship. Belonging as full-fledged encounter.

The landscapes I sought to record never failed to live up to the tourist images of Alps and sapphire blue lakes I had grown to know so well. The brand of Switzerland imprinted in my mind was easily recognizable so that it was sometimes difficult to take even the most stunning scenery seriously.

While I was often overwhelmed by the intensity of the images I was hiking through, I was also aware of the challenge of perceiving them. Just as I had once struggled to describe my first experience of Switzerland without falling into a chapter of *Heidi*, I now felt I was gazing at mountains like models arranged for the glossy pages of a travel magazine.

How is it that a cliché contains truth yet is a complete misrepresentation?

My attention to sensation over story was in part my effort to overcome a blind observation of beauty. In order to write the place as it was in relation to my body, I had to be present to both. Rather than standing outside looking in, I had to experience myself, as Merleau-Ponty puts it, embedded in the very world I was writing.

Each canton I explored had a well-developed identity. If Schwyz´s self-conception was that they were the original Switzerland, the canton from which, after all, the country´s very name and flag had originated from, then Uri was the soul and strength of it.

Although I did my best to avoid hearing the stereotypes attached to each place, I couldn´t help but notice a person´s roll of the eyes when I mentioned the manicured gardens in Schwyz, a region known for being rich and conservative, or the chuckle when I talked about the dark walls of Uri, a place often belittled for being as narrow-minded as the valleys by which it is formed. It was only about Unterwalden that people remained strangely silent.

As much as possible, I tried to shed these hints of preconceptions in order to immerse myself in the landscapes themselves. I was curious if any differences between the neighboring areas would appear, or if their particularities were only a matter of cultural imagination.

As the impressions of each canton took written shape, I was surprised by the distinctions appearing on the page, Schwyz´s blooming beauty sharply contrasted by the wildness of Uri´s rugged terrain. Far from lacking character, each of the canton´s singularities came through the text, always emerging in relation of one to the other.

Only in Unterwalden, the borders were quicker to blur. It was as if, even after all these years, the land never completed the divide into the two half cantons of Obwalden and Nidwalden, a political split officially made in 1340.

While the imposing mountain backs of Uri rarely let me forget where I was, in Unterwalden, it was hard to remember. Here borders wandered languidly through spacious valleys and halfway up hills only to descend again into wide stretches of green.

Like a shadow disrupting form, it kept the clarity of the others always in question.

It has been more than two years since I completed the 21 hikes through the cantons. As the details of each place fade back between the gridlines of the map, I´m not sure I belong any more or any less to Switzerland.

I constructed a protocol where there was none. I wrote myself into a narrative and out again.

I paved my own path of initiation.

I believed.

I followed borders, I memorized them, I walked until my tired legs ached with the conviction of each canton, but my student visa still expires in four and a half months.

It is comforting for me to think that in the chosen constitution of this country, the pronouns get confused. In the space between „we“ and „they“, the self is always slipping over the borders of the other, as if a quality of foreignness is a prerequisite to proper relationship, to what it means to belong.

SCHWYZ

I am suddenly very small in a land of deep, deep valleys, as if the landscape has lifted and poured me into itself, the lake is gone, and I am enveloped by mountains. With farms scattered down the steep slopes, I am held in on every side by walls of green, a green so intense that it resists the eye. The color hovers and rises off the grass like ripples of heat.

Before this moment, before the place becomes a minor obsession, before my ears tune to the name like to the mention of a hidden crush, the canton does not exist for me. I´m lost the first time I wander into Schwyz. I cross an invisible border and I emerge into the presence of a place.

From my home in Basel, on the border of Switzerland, I begin to make weekly visits to the interior canton of the country. Each Saturday, rising in the dark, I braid my hair, lather myself in sunscreen and tie up the laces of my boots before catching the early morning tram to the station.

Week by week, train ride by train ride, trail by trail, the canton begins to appear.

Along the shores of Sihlsee, a plume of smoke rises from a distant stretch of sand. It is a still morning, and the burning wood fills the air with a fragrance of incense like cedar and myrrh. The shades and shapes of houses reflect across the lake, a mirror of watercolor, and beyond the shore, the hills rise beneath blankets of green.

A tractor drives up a dirt road leading to a dark wooden storehouse. A calico cat lies on the pavement and rolls over in the sun.

Fields turn to forest as a path ascends the base of a bordering mountain. My calves ache with the first efforts of the day. My breath quickens; my heart begins to pound.

In the nave of a cathedral, wooden pews shrink beneath walls of glaring white stucco. The ceiling caves upward into a dark dome of frescoed angels as they descend through black storm clouds.

The sanctuary is filled with statues of saints, like a witch´s lair, where every enemy has been turned to stone. St. Agatha stands with her severed breasts balanced on a golden plate, while at her feet, a skeleton reclines in a glass casket, propped on one elbow with his fingers adorned in jewels.

Above the pews, a pulpit of rose-colored marble etched in gold is held aloft by four stone figures, young men with bent necks whose backs are bowed beneath the weight. Rippled veins appear along the muscles of their arms. With their arched soles suspended just above my head, I envy the solidity of each marble toe flexed with life.

Drapes of snow disappear into crevices as they melt into the thunder of waterfalls. Beneath the late afternoon sunlight, the sea green of the lower rock brightens and fades; the colors shift like a kaleidoscope of jade shadows.

I begin to anticipate my trips to Schwyz like a drug I grow anxious without. I study the map, and with each unfolding, I discover new areas where my routes have yet to reach.

My exploration of Schwyz is less about conquest than entreaty. Each week I make a pilgrimage to the center of the country and I ask to be let in.

A jagged horizon of white wilderness rises far above a lake where a cloak of azure wraps around the base of the mountains.

The surface breaks beneath my boot. I hear the crunch of snow crystals and my foot disappears into a hollow below. I take another step into the carpet of white, and through my wool socks, flakes of ice begin to melt against my skin.

From a signature steeple, the bells ring on the hour, drowning out the clatter of cowbells. On the main street stand a Coop, a bakery, a post office, a house with the lace curtains closed.

Beyond the high fields, where a farmer is cutting hay, lie the manicured grass squares of a golf course where carts glide along paved paths and men wear visors to shield their eyes from the glare of the snow-ridged skyline. Yellow signs caution hikers to watch out for flying golf balls.

A cloud moves across the sun – the view grows darker, more acute – as I watch the lower landscapes interlock like a puzzle coming together before my eyes. I scan from the peak of the *Grosser Mythen* to the black forested hills which lead to Einsiedeln to the shores of Sihlsee, where weeks ago I sat on the rocks and listened to the lapping of waves against the roar of traffic and the distant song of Alphorns.

At a trailhead near Muotathal, I see the name *Hölloch* carved into a wooden sign with a red arrow pointing into the woods. A nearby plaque explains that *Hölloch*, translated as „hellhole“, is a cave just over 200 kilometers long and reaching nearly one thousand meters deep beneath the mountainous terrain. Below the panel of warped plastic is an image of visitors smiling beneath their orange helmets as they enjoy wine and raclette in the candlelit glow of a cavern. For a substantial fee, an unforgettable experience is promised to „outdoor lovers of all ages“.

The cave is closed for the season, but for the rest of the day, through high valleys and along ridges overlooking snow-chiseled peaks, I cannot stop thinking about the vast interior beneath my feet.

It is late spring, and the city is in bloom. Clouds float across a bright sky and the air is fragrant with the scent of shaggy white blossoms adorning the trees. Cobblestone streets lead through manor houses with red geraniums in the windowsills overlooking garden rows with wings of chard and leaves of cabbages unfurled.

In the center of the town, beneath the shadow of a cathedral's spire, there is a small chapel with a heavy wooden door. Inside, awaiting burial, an old man lies in a coffin. A frame of his smiling photograph sits nearby, yet the powdered features of his face are almost unrecognizable. The thin eyelids and pale lips have been shut and all facial hair removed from the doll-like skin now softened and smoothed.

I walk within deep grooves furrowed into the earth. Walls of sweet-smelling foliage rise as high as my shoulders on each side until the embankment ebbs away into a wide-open meadow of white and yellow wildflowers. Cows graze in the tall grass swaying beneath the cherry trees.

It is a holiday weekend and the trail is teeming with tourists. At every bend in the path, pristine vistas of Alps and glacial lakes appear within polished frames of forest and sky. I stare at the mountains. I take pictures to prove their reality, but the distant figures appear on my phone as a panorama of hazy white shadows.

I strain to listen to the wind in the trees over the murmur of conversation ahead and behind me. I try to feel the weight of my boots as they scuff across hardened patches of snow.

Hours pass and after I´ve made a few false turns on the trail, the tourists are gone. I realize I am alone on the wrong side of the mountain and the fastest direction to follow is down. I let gravity carry me as I leave the trail and bound through the grass, zig-zagging down the hillside toward a lake the color of sky.

URI

In the beginning, I inch toward Uri. I am not in a hurry to leave the newfound familiarity of Schwyz with its rolling pastures and blossoming trees where I once walked past a herd of bleating goats, who, in place of bells, wore tinkling wind chimes around their necks.

Uri´s coat of arms, often painted on the surface of a boulder along a road or off the beaten track, is a fierce black bull set against a stark yellow flag. The beast is recognizable by its narrowed eyes, a protruding red tongue and a heavy ring hanging from its nose.

I put off the journey, I delay, but immersion into one canton is not complete without immersion into the other, like the rings of a labyrinth, each circle enclosed and enclosing, until one is held within the center.

On a headstone with no name, a bearded man with thick windblown hair leans out of the rock and lifts his sculpted face to the mountains beyond his grave.

When I arrive to Erstfeld, the sun has just begun its descent behind the valley´s dark walls. I immediately check the train departures back to Basel. Stopping to buy a cup of coffee at the kiosk, I ask the woman behind the counter where the old town is. She smiles, a little amused. „This is it", she says.

I step out of the train station into an empty street where I´m watched by every stranger I pass. I walk faster to escape observation, past windows of crocheted curtains and plastic figures of red-hooded gnomes, but before I have even finished my cup of coffee, I am at the end of town and walking down a highway to nowhere.

„Danke und auf Wiedersehen", the yellow sign reads.

A mountain peak rises, disappears and then resurfaces from a sea of fog. Like a presence taking up the fullness of a room, its form is felt even when hidden in a shroud.

From each side of a ridge, waves of white wash toward the path and form a triangular corridor through which three hikers pass. A moment later, they are engulfed in the grey, and I can only hear their bodiless voices ahead of me.

Tracing the river, like a steel shadow, railroad tracks interlock across the valley floor. Rows of dull red train cars with blunted square faces rest motionless on the tracks facing the threshold of the Gotthard tunnel.

The trail refuses to skim the surface of the land; it cuts straight through the rutted earth so that I am stepping over rocks and roots emerging from the ground. Waterfalls spill across the path, and the trail does not lead around the cow pastures but through them. I cannot get used to the immensity of those heavy brown bodies so near me, the thick protruding bones of their backsides, and their short sharp horns, as they languidly watch me tiptoe by.

Thick plates of snow lie broken and melting. Between their saw-like edges, a stream flows under the hollows of remaining snow.

Cutting around a blind corner, the bus´s weight leans toward a cliff and the three-tone horn blares, sounding like something between a dying Alphorn and a slow ambulance. Another bend, and the window scrapes against a wall of jutted rock. There is a murmur of gasps and nervous laughter as the bus regains its balance and disappears into a black hole blasted through the side of the mountain. The tunnel opens again above a ravine of gushing water with Jurassic-sized boulders breaking its flow.

The stone foundation of a chalet seems to have grown into the hillside, and the roof is merged with a layer of green earth drawn over the house like a blanket.

Fog hangs between crags of rock deep with crevices. The charcoal clefts descend to high banks of lime-painted grass, almost fluorescent against the gray.

I am walking across a plateau of smoky white stone. The pale floor is flecked with dark moss, and the hard surface has smooth indents like large fingerprints pressed into clay. Between the cracks, clusters of grass grow from the damp seaweed-colored ground. The air is pungent with the smell of earth.

Clambering across a landslide of boulders and broken shale, I can almost feel the rumble and crash of rocks as I stumble across the standstill.

One night before I leave for Uri, I lie in bed hugging a pillow to my chest. For days now, there is a dull aching throb. As I turn off the light, I can hear the alarm already ringing in my ears. I pull the covers close and my legs grow heavy as I trace the morning´s journey in my mind.

The forecast says there will be thunderstorms.

A small brown snake appears on the trail. It shakes its tongues and then slithers away.

I sit up in bed and pull on jeans, a sports bra, a tank top, a hoodie. I scoop coffee grounds into the stovetop funnel. I fill my water bottle. I stack slices of bread and cheese and place them in a plastic bag. I swab sunscreen like warpaint onto my face. I braid my hair between gulps of coffee and then pull on my boots and walk out the door. My body resents being jolted across the pavement as I run, just in time to slip through the closing tram door.

A canyon opens between two mountains and surging with strength, a river appears. The greenish-gray water whirls forward into rapids of white.

High up the wooded mountainside, I see a chain of waterfalls, not as trickling streams slowly gaining strength, but as full-fledged rivers leaping off cliffs amid clouds of mist.

Holding my breath against the smell of exhaust mingled with the stench of tar, I follow a trail along the railroad tracks. The path leads me against the direction of traffic far below where cars inch toward the Gotthard Tunnel. I can barely hear the nearby river or the persistent cicadas over the drone of cars, and yet the presence of the thoroughfare does not feel like a disruption to the landscape, but a strange evolution of the raw power of this place.

The sky darkens as the sun disappears behind ash clouds. As if the landscape has been put under a filter, the rolling green deepens and brightens; the contrast of every contour is made visible, like the ragged edges of earth where the carpet has been torn in two allowing the pale water to flow through.

At a cable car station, through a thin wooden door and up the stairs, the small white bathroom is washed in sunlight, and the window is cracked so the cool morning air can come through. A fresh towel hangs beside the sink and there is a full bottle of soap.

Grey stone pyramids lift against a blue sky, while fog rises like incense above the plains.

Inside the door of a mountain hut, a wooden shelf, standing against a rock wall, is filled from floor to ceiling with rubber clogs, each pair carefully arranged with the heel of one fitted into the toe of the other. Like a box of Crayola crayons, the house shoes are organized with a shelf for every color: white, mint green, pink, orange and three shades of blue.

I walk past the shelf of shoes and into an empty dining room where rustic chandeliers hang above long tables lined by chairs with thick carved backs. Faded paintings of Alps hang on the wooden walls, beside lace-framed windows revealing a similar view.

Walking into a wall of fog, I withdraw my hands into my sleeves and pull up my hoodie. A chill blows across the bare ground.

It has been a four-hour journey from Basel after a night of very little sleep, but I am wide awake after the bus´s ascent up the mountain. The tightly twisted road had risen higher and higher, and when I thought we had reached the top, the sun just then breaking through, the bus climbed even higher still until I was watching birds circle the air below me, and above, serrated tusks of rock emerge out of a clouded sky.

At the trailhead, another hiker laments the impressive view now masked in fog, but I am relieved to be blinded, already weary of feeling inadequate to all of the beauty below.

By the time I have reached the bottom of the sloping bowl formed by the surrounding mountains, I become aware of the pain which has been building in my knees. The relief of a flat gravel road is short-lived, as it leads to a further descent of two thousand meters. My knees tremble each time my foot touches the ground and the sharpness of the pain stops me every few meters. I try walking sideways, I try walking off-trail to cushion my steps with mounds of grass, I try walking without bending my legs, but my knees are beyond consolation.

When I arrive back to Basel late that night, I hobble off the train, bewildered by the extent of my defeat.

Along a main street, the large forepaws of a bear hang from two chains in a showcase window. Tufts of fur remain at the base of the thick claws, but the creased skin is grey with age. A nearby plaque informs me that these are the remnants of the last bear to be shot in the valley.

The air is white and motionless. The ground is matted in damp leaves, brown and yellow with flecks of dying green. The path opens onto a bow of land reaching into a void of fog where treetops surface like shadows. For a moment, the veil thins and a rockface, immense and startlingly close, appears at my side.

I hear footsteps behind me. I turn and see the first hiker I have met all day, a pale man in his thirties wearing an army green jacket. He has a shaggy beard and black hair that is cut like a bowl around his head. He avoids my eyes and says nothing as we pass. I walk faster as I feel for the pocket-knife in my coat. For the rest of the trail, my pace is unrelenting through misty woods of bone-thin trees. I glance back at every turn but the path disappears into fog. I hurry on, walking through wisps of cloud as they float across the trail.

The trunks of the trees are hairy with moss and diverge into fingerlike roots, digging themselves into the ground.

Within the warmth of a chapel, a tall candle flickers beside a small coffin. The dripping wax is decorated with colorful stick figures of children, each holding the others′ hands, as they form a ring around the base of fire. On the wall above, a crucifix with a loincloth of gold is accompanied by figures of mournful saints and fierce angels who seem to stand guard over the dead.

As I inch toward the open frame, I am already imagining the childlike corpse evoked by the rainbow colors of the candle. My heart is thumping in my chest. I lean my face forward and take a step closer even as my body draws back. The inside of the coffin comes into view, empty and waiting.

Above the trail, giant wind chimes swing from a tree, each chime the size of a small baseball bat. The metal tubes have lost their tune and clank together like a jostled toolset.

UNTERWALDEN
(Nidwalden, Obwalden)

On a Saturday morning on the shores of Vierwaldersee, hot water bottles in knitted sweaters are for sale outside the local Drogerie. The fog encloses the town like a morning robe and hangs low over the water as waves gently lap over pebbles alongside the empty boardwalk. Indoors, people gather at the bakery with its long wooden tables beneath warm lighting and floral-printed walls hung with black-and-white photos of women eyeing elaborately decorated cakes.

I am on my first trip to Nidwalden where my initial impression is a striking absence of canton flags. I walk through town and see no more than a little red cloth waving from a flower pot.

In the weeks that follow, I try to pay attention to the borders between Nidwalden and Obwalden, but it is difficult to explore one canton without slipping into the other. Even the barrier of a mountain range between the two valleys is inconclusive. I board a cable car in Obwalden, float halfway up a mountain and step out in Nidwalden where the sharp edges of the snowy summit are washed out against a white sky.

It is early evening and the forested slopes of a gorge glimmer in hues of crimson and gold. A monastery is tucked into the trees far below and leading up from the riverbed, a monk walks along the path deep in conversation with another man. His dark robes sway with the slow rhythm of his movement.

From the veranda of a luxury hotel overlooking the ravine, guests stand shivering and smoking, occasionally glancing up at the portrait of the Alps framed by the valley´s fertile walls.

On the morning train to Stans, I sit next to an elderly woman dressed in a bright red pantsuit. She regularly leans forward to make comments to her companion, a woman who cannot hear well and must ask her friend to repeat every statement with a strained but patient smile. Soon the old woman gives up the conversation and turns to me. When she realizes I don't speak Swiss-German, she is undeterred. Her dense wrinkles merge into a grin as she says my two braids make me look just like Gretel from the fairytale. I am surprised by the suggestion, more often told I look like Heidi.

I am walking through curtains of yellow leaves.

Stretches of green carpet the valley floor, a floor so wide, it is easy for me to forget I am in a valley at all. From the train station, smooth level streets unroll themselves in the sun, past a woman who nods and smiles at me from the porch of her yellow house, past an old man bent over the tangled vines of his garden. He glances up and greets a girl waving from her bicycle as she rides by.

I have the nagging impression I am walking through the set of a movie, but as a woman stops to ask if I need directions, I find the details of the place thoroughly convincing. The air is cool and fragrant with the familiar scent of freshly sheared hay and the burning wood of a nearby fire.

Stripped branches form an arch over the trail. Last slips of yellow hang suspended among the trees like confetti caught mid-air. On the ground, beneath a layer of amber- and copper -colored leaves, the carpet has turned jet black.

I can feel the bare hills rolling softly, their sides of wooly green so large and close; they are like sleeping creatures breathing beside me.

The bus to Oberrickenbach is barely a bus, but instead a small van waiting at the station. It is empty except for the bearded driver studying his hands while listening to the buoyant tunes of an accordion on the radio. As he starts the engine, he looks at me through the rearview mirror and says the cable car in Oberrickenbach is closed. Then he turns up the music and we are soon zigzagging up the mountain.

By the time we reach the village, there is yodeling on the radio. The van is halted by a herd of sheep crossing the street as a tractor lumbers ahead in the distance. Through the window, I see a farmer rolling logs, one by one, down a steep hillside.

Fog envelops silver fields stiff with ice, each stem, leaf and petal outlined in crystal white.

As if emerging out of a grayscale photograph into a world of color, I step out of the misty woods to see the fog quickly washing down the mountainside, a retreating flood radiant with the rising sun. Within seconds, a panorama of the Alps unveils itself around me. I am at the foot of lofty walls and towering pinnacles, colossal figures that only a moment before had been nothing more than faint shadows in the fog.

Just below the range of mountains, stands a wall of earth, and from the other side, surfacing as if out of a void I cannot see, waves of cloud rise up and roll across the crest. I follow the trail along the wall and realize I am looking at the barrier of a dam carved into a bowl of mountains with the clouds doing somersaults across the dark water where the sun has yet to reach.

Pop music plays on speakers in the snowy parking lot and the smash hits follow me through the automatic doors to the ticket booth, to the bathroom, to the long dim hall with pink techno lights leading to the slowly circulating gondolas.

I step carefully into the small hanging room. *Titlis*, the golden logo of the mountain, is printed across the back of the black carpeted seat beneath an outline of a wave-like summit. I am still alone when the doors close and the gondola glides forward, lifting silently into the air. The ski season has yet to officially open and there are at least twenty empty gondolas floating by, each with a flag of a different country, or canton.

On a still morning, a solitary tree is raining dead leaves,
the branches steadily showering the path as if seized by a
moment of release long after the wind has gone.

A day descends into a glow of blue behind a peak swept
in a halo of light. Wisps of snow blow from the tip,
curling before dissolving and drifting away.
As if for the first time, I inhale.
My breath fills my lungs.

The sun is a white globe mirrored in the black marble of a lake. Sheets of ice spread to the center where the depth is enclosed beneath the reflection of mountains. Each crease, each ripple of surrounding rock is brushed in snow, and the persistent roar of a machine producing the pale vapor pursues me along the trail.

It takes a long time before the gondola station and scattered huts are hidden behind the Stracciatella-colored hills, and all I can hear are the crunch of my footsteps and the padded hood of my jacket rustling against my ears.

Within a circling horizon of jagged Alps, paths curve along silky dunes of white powder. My eyes ache with the brightness of the ground as I keep my gaze on the clumsy tread of my snowshoes. Each plunge sends flakes flying and sparkling into the air.

A flock of white birds glides over a village, over the metal warehouses, the train station, the tractors, the stacks of apartments, the cathedral´s open doors with the floor-length curtains pulled aside to let the wind pass through.

The birds are a slow silent wave of bodies moving up and down before diverging into two spheres. Form holds, wavers and then disperses into the grey air as drops of rain begin to fall.

EINLEITUNG

„Bevor ich dreissig Jahre lang Zen studierte, hatte ich Berge als Berge und Flüsse als Flüsse gesehen. Als ich ein besseres Verständnis entwickelte, gelangte ich an den Punkt, an dem ich sah, dass Berge nicht Berge sind und Flüsse nicht Flüsse. Jetzt aber, da ich in der Ruhe beheimatet bin, sage ich: Berge sind wirklich Berge und Flüsse wirklich Flüsse."

Ch'ing-yüan Wei-hsin

Bevor ich eine Rolle in der Geschichte spielte – bevor ich ein Visum, einen Job, einen Freundeskreis, eine Wohnung hatte; bevor ich mich in einen Schweizer verliebte und dadurch rechtfertigen konnte, warum ich hier bin, wurde ich oft gefragt:

Warum bist du hier?

Warum die Schweiz?

Ich wusste nicht, wie ich das Gefühl beschreiben sollte, nach Hause zu kommen.

Mein Ur-Grossvater war ein Schweizer, der sein Land aber seit langem verlassen hatte. Und auch wenn ich seine Geschichte romantisierte, um meine Wurzeln hier zu rechtfertigen, gab es doch keine klare Herkunft. Ich hatte auch Vorfahren in Frankreich, Deutschland, England und anderswo.

Eines Tages stolperte ich im Schweizer Gesetzbuch über einen Artikel zur Einbürgerung mit dem Titel „Irrtümliche Annahme des Schweizer Bürgerrechts".

Wer während fünf Jahren im guten Glauben gelebt hat, das Schweizer Bürgerrecht zu besitzen, und während dieser Zeit von kantonalen oder Gemeindebehörden tatsächlich als Schweizerin oder als Schweizer behandelt worden ist, kann ein Gesuch um erleichterte Einbürgerung stellen.

Zuerst lachte ich, beinahe hoffnungsvoll. Ein Gesetz, das auf Glauben beruht, schien mir absurd. Meine Recherche ergab, dass der Artikel in der Praxis selten angewandt wird. Die Idee scheint zu den Ideen der Reformation zu passen. In den Augen der damaligen religiösen Bewegung hatte der Papst als Vermittler der Erlösung keine Autorität. Die Macht des Glaubens war wichtiger als gute Taten.

Wenn man das Heil durch Glauben erlangen kann, warum nicht auch Nationalität? Was, wenn ich auf die Frage, warum ich hier bin, einfach antworten würde: Weil ich glaube.

Etymologisch betrachtet, geht das englische Verb *belong*, zu deutsch *(hin- oder an-) gehören*, auf das späte 14. Jahrhundert zurück und wurde verwendet, um Eigentum zu bezeichnen: „das Eigentum von“ oder „ein Mitglied von“ zu sein. Zugehörigkeit ist entsprechend nur möglich, wenn die Bedingungen des Besitzes festgelegt und die Grenzen der Zugehörigkeit klar gezogen sind. Was festgelegt ist, tritt in Kraft. Wenn die Grenzen feststehen, bekommen wir einen Platz. Wir gehören dazu.

An meinem ersten Morgen in der Schweiz wachte ich spät im Haus eines entfernten Verwandten auf. Kühle Luft drang durch das Fenster und noch bevor ich meine Augen öffnete, konnte ich die feuchte Erde riechen und das frische Gras nach dem Regen.

Ich drehte mich nur einmal kurz um in der Nacht, als ich unter der warmen Daunendecke das leise Trommeln auf dem Dach hörte.

Mein Gastgeber war lange vor mir wach und so kam ich die hölzerne Treppe hinunter in eine leere Küche, wo ein eiserner Teekrug auf mich wartete, warmgehalten durch eine Kerze. Daneben lagen auf einem Holzbrett ein Stück Brot und verschiedene Sorten Käse. Feste, würzige Blöcke und süsse, weisse Scheiben, weicher als Butter.

In der Ferne konnte ich den Donner über den Alpen hören. Gegenüber im Tal waren die Gipfel in Wolken gehüllt, dennoch konnte ich die Umrisse ihrer mächtigen Gestalt ausmachen.

Ich war damals knapp 21 und wollte eigentlich nur drei Monate in Europa bleiben. Aber dann verschob ich mein Unistudium und schob die Ausreise aus der Schweiz immer wieder hinaus. Ständig aus- und wieder einreisend, ständig in leichter Panik, ob mein Touristen-Visum noch einmal verlängert wird, und immer mit dem Gefühl von Heimweh, sobald ich die Schweiz wieder verliess.

Mein Körper, der nichts von den Einreisebestimmungen wusste, liess sich schon viel früher hier nieder. Meine Schultern entspannten sich, mein Atem wurde tiefer, mein ganzer Körper wurde schwer, als ob ich das erste Mal festen Boden unter den Füssen spürte. In einem Land, in dem ich Ausländerin war, fühlte ich den irrationalen Impuls, Wurzeln zu schlagen.

Irgendwann gingen mir die Ausreden aus, hier zu bleiben, während meine Familie, Freunde und ein angenehmes Leben in den Staaten auf mich wartete. Aber mit diesem tiefen Gefühl, angekommen zu sein, wehrte ich mich gegen alles, was mich wieder wegzog. Jung und hungrig nach einem Zuhause, war ich bereit, alle nötigen Bestimmungen zu befolgen und jedes Initiations-Ritual zu absolvieren, das von mir verlangt wurde.

Es dauerte Jahre, bis ich verstand, dass es diese gab. Die Antwort auf die Frage, ob ich in die Schweiz gehöre, war ganz einfach: Ich tat es nicht.

Ich bin in den Vereinigten Staaten mit dem Mythos aufgewachsen, dass alle, die in das Land kamen, hart arbeiteten und an den amerikanischen Traum glaubten, Leute von uns waren. Amerikaner*in zu werden hing von der Fähigkeit ab, allen Widrigkeiten zum Trotz – institutionalisierter Rassismus, Armut, körperlicher Schmerz –, erfolgreich zu sein, wobei jedes Hindernis durch schiere Tapferkeit überwunden werden konnte. Ein Erfolg, den die Nation dann für sich verbuchen konnte.

Egal, ob eine Einwanderin mit offenen Armen empfangen wurde oder unter erschwerten Bedingungen hier gelandet ist, entscheidend war, dass er oder sie felsenfest davon überzeugt war, dass alles möglich ist. Nur wer diese Feuerprobe bestand, war es wert, in das grossartigste Land der Welt aufgenommen zu werden.

In den 1920er Jahren ist mein Urgrossvater diesem Mythos gefolgt. Zwischen 1890 und 1930 wanderten etwa 90 000 Schweizer Bürger*innen in die Vereinigten Staaten aus. Unter ihnen mein 17-jähriger Urgrossvater und seine Brüder. Land war billig, die industrialisierte Landwirtschaft wuchs, und in einer Zeit, in der Fremdenfeindlichkeit weit verbreitet war, hatte es Vorteile, ein weisser europäischer Mann zu sein. Mein Urgrossvater, der auf der Suche nach Arbeit nach Amerika gekommen war, begann mit Feldarbeit, machte allmählich Karriere als Ingenieur und wurde schliesslich internationaler Vertreter für Caterpillar-Traktoren.

Fast ein Jahrhundert später interessierte sich in der Schweiz niemand dafür, wie entschlossen ich war, zu bleiben. Niemand hatte ein Ohr für dramatische Erzählungen über den Aufstieg und das erträumte Leben. Auf der Einwanderungsbehörde versicherte man mir, ich sei kein Einzelfall. In den USA wäre ich eine von Hunderttausenden von Bürgerinnen mit Schweizer Wurzeln.

Was meine Zugehörigkeit betrifft, war die Sachlage eindeutig. Ich bin Amerikanerin, weil mein Urgrossvater den dummen Fehler begangen hat, seine Heimat zu verlassen.

Als ich schliesslich doch in die USA zurückkehrte, um mein Studium abzuschliessen, fühlte ich mich dort wie in einem emotionalen Exil, weit weg von der Wahlheimat, die mich nicht haben wollte. Ich studierte Kreatives Schreiben und schrieb lange, elegische Erzählungen über meine Vorfahren. Ich fand und erfand immer wieder neue Gründe, warum ich in die Schweiz gehörte. Obwohl meine Argumente nicht schlüssig waren, nickten meine Klassenkamerad*innen verständnisvoll mit dem Kopf. Schliesslich las ich in der Bibliothek stapelweise alte Bücher über die Schweizer Geschichte, als ob das Studium der Wurzeln des andern Landes mir etwas darüber beibringen können würde, wie ich meine eigenen veredeln konnte.

In der Geschichtsschreibung steht, dass die Schweizerische Eidgenossenschaft 1291 aus den drei benachbarten Waldkantonen Schwyz, Uri und Unterwalden gegründet wurde. Die drei lokalen Regierungen wollten ein Bündnis gegen die Habsburger Oberherren schliessen, die sich der Region am Gotthard näherten.

Anfang August soll an den Hängen des Seelisbergs, die zum Vierwaldstättersee hinunterführen, ein Gelöbnis stattgefunden haben, bei dem drei Männer, je ein Vertreter jedes Kantons, einen Schwur zum Schutz ihrer Freiheit leisteten. Ähnliche Verträge zwischen den Kantonen hatte es schon früher gegeben, doch der Bundesbrief von 1291 ist einer der ältesten, der schriftlich festgehalten und aufbewahrt wurde.

Wie üblich war der Text wahrscheinlich ein Flickwerk anderer Verträge, die zu einem eigenen Dokument zusammengefügt wurden. Es ist voller Rechtschreibfehler und Unstimmigkeiten, wie z. B. Verschiebungen und Wechsel der Pronomen „wir" und „sie". Der Text wurde nicht unterschrieben und enthält keinerlei Hinweis darauf, wer anwesend war oder an welchem Ort der Pakt geschlossen wurde.

Das Manuskript war bis 1758 in den Schwyzer Archiven verschollen, und selbst heute weiss niemand genau, wie alt es eigentlich ist. Erst gegen Ende des 19. Jahrhunderts machte die Regierung das unbedeutende Dokument zur verfassungsmässigen Geburtsurkunde der Schweiz.
Als der politische Druck in den 1930er Jahren in Europa zunahm, wurde der Schweiz die Dringlichkeit einer kohärenten Identität bewusst. Ein öffentliches Image, mit der sie der veränderten Welt entgegentreten konnte. Der Bundesbrief und somit die Geschichte vom mutigen Widerstand dreier Kantone

gegen fremde Mächte wurde so zum Symbol der Freiheit und Unabhängigkeit. Lange nach dem legendären Schwur im Jahr 1291 teilte sich Unterwalden in die beiden Halbkantone Obwalden und Nidwalden. Zwanzig weitere Kantone und vier Halbkantone schlossen sich der Eidgenossenschaft an und bildeten die heutige Schweiz.

Ob Fakt oder Fiktion, Schwyz, Uri und Unterwalden repräsentieren historisch den Kerns des Landes; hier haben sich die ersten Wurzeln gebildet.

Zwischen Mitte Zwanzig und Anfang dreissig schloss ich mein Studium ab und reiste von einem Schreib-Stipendium zum nächsten. Doch die Schweiz blieb ein festes Ziel. Ich besuchte sie so oft wie möglich und plante, bei der ersten Gelegenheit zurückzukehren.

Freunde und Familie begegneten meiner andauernden Beschäftigung mit der Schweiz mit leichter Sorge. War es Nostalgie? War ich auf der Suche nach einem bestimmten Gemütszustand? Was projizierte ich auf das Land? Oder wollte ich einfach nur das, was ich nicht haben konnte?

Natürlich habe ich mich dasselbe gefragt.

Dass ich meine Obsession nicht mal mir selbst erklären konnte, war mir keine Hilfe. Wenn ich gefragt wurde, was mich gerade an der Schweiz derart faszinierte, zucke ich wegen meiner eigenen Erklärungen innerlich zusammen. Meine Worte klangen, als stammten sie direkt aus den Buchseiten von *Heidi*. Eine sentimentale Geschichte über ein Waisenmädchen, das mit seinem Grossvater ein neues Leben in den Schweizer Bergen findet. Sie verbringt ihre Tage damit, durch Edelweiss-Wiesen zu laufen, während Ziegen hinter ihr hüpfen. In der Mitte der Geschichte muss sie in die Stadt ziehen, wo sie so sehr an Heimweh erkrankt, dass der Arzt keine andere Lösung sieht, als Heidi in die Alpen zurückkehren zu lassen.

Trotz meiner Entfremdung vom Heimatland war ich gesund. Mein Grossvater wartete nicht auf mich. Und so gab es

Zeiten, in denen selbst ich versuchte, mich von der Illusion eines Lebens in der Schweiz zu lösen.

In Seattle fand ich mit einer Freundin ein leicht verfallenes, aber charmantes Haus in einem Quartier, das wir liebten. Und so beschloss ich, dass es Zeit war, meine jugendlichen Träume beiseitezulegen und mich in der Schönheit dieses temporären Zuhauses einzurichten. Ich wollte den Rat der anderen befolgen, mich nicht länger woanders hin wünschen, sondern anfangen, meinen kleinen Freundeskreis in dieser wundervollen Stadt zu schätzen.

Am Tag, an dem ich diesen Vorsatz gefasst hatte, kam meine Mitbewohnerin in die Küche, und verkündete, dass wir zwangsgeräumt werden würden; das Haus sollte abgerissen werden. Eine Welle der Erleichterung überkam mich. Ich begann sofort, Pläne zu schmieden für etwas, von dem ich hoffte, dass es, ob richtig oder falsch, mein endgültiger Umzug nach Europa sein würde.

Ein Jahr lang habe ich gespart und bei Freunden auf der Couch übernachtet, und flog schliesslich in die Schweiz. Dort habe ich die nächsten zweieinhalb Jahre damit verbracht, ein Visum zu besorgen, damit ich im Land oder zumindest auf dem Kontinent bleiben konnte, bis ich schliesslich einen Platz in einem Masterstudiengang in Zürich bekam. Nachdem ich den elegischen Essay ausgeschöpft hatte, war ich entschlossen, eine neue Form zu finden, in der ich mich in die Geschichte des Landes einschreiben konnte.

Schon lange hatte ich nach einer Möglichkeit gesucht, die körperliche Dimension der Sprache besser zu verstehen. Ich war Autorin, mein Medium war das Wort, aber ich hatte oft die Körperlichkeit anderer Disziplinen beneidet. Während andere Künstlerinnen ihre Objekte bewegten, bauten, malten und skulptierten, sass ich am Computer und tippte Ideen.

Zwar war mir bewusst, dass es nicht möglich war, etwas so Immaterielles, wie einen Gedanken oder ein Gefühl zu beschreiben. Dem Philosophen John Dewey nach, gibt es Angst oder Liebe an sich nicht. Es gibt nur die spezifischen Umstände, die sie hervorrufen. Jedes Gefühl hat seine Wurzeln in einer spezifischen, physischen Eigenart eines Augenblicks – der physischen Besonderheit eines Ortes.

Als ich zum ersten Mal in der Schweiz ankam, hatte sich mein Körper in den Boden eingegraben, lange bevor meinem Gehirn eine gute Theorie einfiel, warum. Wie sollte ich also das Gefühl dieses Landes beschreiben? Was waren die sensorischen Details meiner ursprünglichen Verbundenheit? Sicherlich war es mehr als Käsestücke und eine heisse Tasse Tee an einem stürmischen Morgen, aber immerhin das.

Ist ein Ort nicht eine Sammlung von Gegenständen, die wir berühren, riechen und schmecken können?

Ich habe mir Schwyz, Uri und Unterwalden zunächst nicht als Orte für meine Integration vorgestellt. Ich hatte die Namen der Kantone längst zwischen den Geschichtsbüchern vergessen, die wieder in der Bibliothek in Seattle standen. Zurück in der Schweiz nahm ich statt Büchern stapelweise Landkarten zur Hand, plante Wanderungen und studierte die Höhenlinien, um mich besser im Gelände zu orientieren.

Es war Anfang Frühling und die Wege begannen unter der Schneeschmelze zu tauen, als ich einen Weg beschritt, der passenderweise Alpenpanoramaweg heisst. Ein Alpenmeer erstreckte sich soweit das Auge reichte. Die Sitzbänke an jedem Aussichtspunkt schienen auf das Staunen der Tourist*innen abgestimmt zu sein. Für kurze Zeit teilte ich die Bewunderung der anderen Wander*innen, doch weil ich versuchte den Menschenmassen aus dem Weg zu gehen, war ich kurz abgelenkt und nahm eine falsche Abzweigung. Endlich allein mit der Landschaft, verirrte ich mich immer mehr, durchquerte Wiesen mit hohem Gras und versuchte, den Weg ins Tal zu finden.

Selbst heute könnte ich wohl den Irrweg, den ich genommen habe, nicht mehr nachvollziehen. Er endete auf dem Grund eines Tals, in dem die Berge nicht mehr nur

Panoramahintergrund waren. Vielmehr spürte ich ihre allesumfassende Präsenz. Die offensichtliche Schönheit der Berge, die sich auf dem Panoramaweg fast banal angefühlt hatte, verschluckte mich komplett.

Es ist schwierig zu erklären, was genau es ist, das einen Ort greifbar macht, warum ein Tal pulsiert, während ein anderes einfach nur flach daliegt. Ich habe versehentlich eine Grenze überschritten und eine Landschaft betreten, die ich nicht mehr ignorieren konnte.

Erst auf der Zugfahrt nach Hause, als ich die Karte vor mir aufklappte, wurde mir klar, dass ich in den Kanton Schwyz gewandert war. Ich hatte ursprünglich vor, von Unterägeri nach Zug zu wandern, war aber auf der falschen Seite des Berges heruntergekommen und am Rande des Ägerisees entlang in ein Tal bei Sattel geraten. Hier hatte sich Schwyz in mir festgesetzt.

Wie konnte es geschehen, dass ich über die Kantonsgrenze stolperte und an diesem neuen Ort landete? Es war nicht das erste Mal, dass ich mich in eine bestimmte Region der Schweiz verliebt hatte. Aber diesmal wollte ich ergründen, warum mich diese Erfahrung so tief berührt hat. War es das Leuchten der späten Nachmittagssonne auf den Talwänden oder die Erleichterung, als ich den Weg den Berg hinunter gefunden hatte und auf ebenem Boden ging. Ob tiefgründig oder trivial, ich wollte mein Erlebnis an diesem Ort ergründen. Vielleicht konnte ich so besser verstehen, warum ich diese tiefe Bindung an ein fremdes Land empfinde. Wenn man mich fragte, warum ich hier bin, wollte ich eine Antwort parat haben. Wenn die Schweiz nicht mehr war als ein Gebilde aus von Menschenhand gezogenen Grenzen, was hielt mich noch in diesem Land, dem ich nie beitreten konnte?

Die Kantone Schwyz, Uri und Unterwalden – wenn vielleicht auch nicht das wahre Herz der Schweiz – symbolisieren sie doch den Moment, wo die Grenzen zum ersten Mal gezogen worden sind. Und ich wollte hier den Zugang zum Selbstverständnis eines Landes finden, das mich nicht einlassen wollte.

In den folgenden neun Monaten unternahm ich 21 Wanderungen, sieben durch jeden der Urkantone. Ich wusste, dass die Gründung ein Mythos war. Dennoch war ich bereit zu glauben, nur um dazuzugehören.

Noch ohne klare Vorstellung, welche Form der Text annehmen würde, habe ich angefangen, scheinbar unbedeutende Ereignisse entlang jedes Weges aufzuschreiben: eine Schlange, die über den Weg gleitet, der Puls meines Herzschlags oder ein Duft von wilder Kamille in der stillen Luft. Ich wollte Worte finden, die so unmittelbar sind, wie die Eindrücke, die mein Körper erfasste. Zum ersten Mal erfuhr ich die Körperlichkeit von Sprache. Und ich schrieb nie weiter, als mich meine Füsse tragen konnten.

Ich erinnere mich, wie ich das vierte, fünfte, sechste Mal mit dem Zug von Basel nach Schwyz fuhr. Es war aufregend immer die gleiche Strecke zu fahren und eine Gleiskurve, ein Heufeld oder das Profil eines Berges wiederzuerkennen. Je häufiger ich hinfuhr, desto mehr dehnte sich die Landschaft aus. Meine wenigen Wanderungen durch einen 907 km^2 grossen Kanton kamen mir wie ein unbeholfener Orientierungsversuch vor.

Wie viele Wanderungen waren nötig, bis es möglich ist, zu sagen, ich kenne einen Ort? Wie viele Wahrzeichen müsste ich identifizieren? Wie viele Dörfer müsste ich benennen können? Je weiter ich meinen Überlegungen nachging, desto absurder wurden sie. Ich machte weiter.

Immer mehr wurde jedes Merkmal, jedes Detail, das ich entdeckte, kostbar vertraut. Landstriche, die auf einer Landkarte nichts weiter als leerer Raum waren, wurden zu einer greifbaren Erfahrung. Ich genoss jeden Eindruck der scharfen Felsen in die Gummisohlen meines Schuhs, selbst meine schmerzenden Knie und sonnenverbrannte Haut, die noch Tage nach meiner Rückkehr von dieser Begegnung erzählten.

In diesem Mikrokosmos der Schweiz verzichtete ich auf die üblichen Wege, um Zugehörigkeit zu erlangen, da mir diese sowieso verwehrt waren. Ich folgte meinem Unterfangen bis zu seinem konsequenten Ende. Ich kam der Schweiz so nahe, dass sich die Beziehung nicht mehr leugnen liess.

Es war ein unverhohlener Versuch der Vereinnahmung durch Intimität.

Die schrittweise Annäherung an die Kantone verfolgte ich auf fast neurotische Weise. Ich musste sehen, wohin mich das führte. Hatte dieses Vorhaben, ein ganzes Land an sich zu reissen, einen Endpunkt?

Eine Neurose ist nach der Definition des *Lexico*-Wörterbuchs: „eine relativ milde psychische Erkrankung, die nicht durch eine organische Krankheit verursacht wird und mit Stresssymptomen (Depression, Angst, zwanghaftes Verhalten...), aber nicht mit einem radikalen Verlust des Realitätssinns einhergeht".

Mein zwanghaftes Verhalten, in jedem Kanton Boden gut zu machen, war getrieben von meiner Sehnsucht, dazuzugehören. Ein radikaler Akt mit der Realität in Berührung zu kommen.

Schritt für Schritt wob ich mich in die Wege ein und lenkte mein Bewusstsein auf Erfahrungssplitter, die ich sonst vielleicht ignoriert hätte. Oft fokussierte ich auf meinen Körper, um den Wind in meinem Nacken zu spüren oder auf das auf meinen Füssen lastende Gewicht, wenn sie durch totes Laub stapften.

Meine Frage war nicht, was Schwyz, Uri oder Unterwalden sind, sondern welche Eigenschaften die Orte hatten, die mit ihren Namen verbunden sind.

Die Antwort, nach der ich suchte, konnte nicht in einem einzelnen Gespräch mit einer Einheimischen oder einer breiten gesellschaftlichen oder gar historischen Analyse gefunden werden. Ich suchte nach etwas urtümlicherem, nach einer vorsprachlichen Beziehung zum Land. Entsprechend folgte ich eher schmalen Pfaden als breiten Strassen und ich zog Kuhweiden Menschenmassen vor.

Das Ziel war nicht mehr, ein objektives Wissen über die Region zu erlangen, sondern vielmehr den verbindenden Fäden nachzuspüren, die mich von einem Moment zum nächsten brachten. Um welche Arten von Beziehung handelt es sich, wenn es um Geschmack, Berührung, Geruch ging – um Sinneseindrücke statt Geschichten?

Es war wohl Teil der Neurose zu glauben, dass jede Grenze eines Kantons oder Landes eine handfeste Realität darstellt, die mich abstossen oder einschliessen würde. Berge sind Berge, Flüsse sind Flüsse, aber jeder Schritt entfernte mich weiter von der finalen Gestalt.

Früher, im 14. Jahrhundert, lange bevor das Wort zur Bezeichnung von Eigentum oder Besitz verwendet wurde, war die ursprüngliche Bedeutung von *belong* „sich angemessen auf etwas zu beziehen". Die Vorsilbe *be-* hat im Altenglischen eine Vielzahl von Bedeutungen, darunter „über, um, auf allen Seiten".

Sich angemessen auf etwas zu beziehen

Zugehörigkeit als Beziehung. Zugehörigkeit durch vollständige Begegnung.

Die Landschaften, die ich festhalten wollte, entsprachen den touristischen Bildern von Alpen und saphirblauen Seen, die ich so gut kennengelernt hatte. Das Klischee der Schweiz in meinem Kopf war leicht wiederzuerkennen, so dass es fast schwierig war, diese beeindruckenden Landschaften ernst zu nehmen.

So sehr ich von der Intensität der Bilder, die ich durchwanderte überwältigt war, war ich mir auch der Herausforderung bewusst, sie wahrzunehmen. So wie ich einst Mühe hatte, mein erstes Erlebnis in der Schweiz zu beschreiben, ohne einer *Heidi*-Vorstellung zu verfallen, so hatte ich nun das Gefühl, dass ich auf die Berge blicke, wie auf Modelle, arrangiert für ein Hochglanzreisemagazin.

Wie kann es sein, dass solch ein Klischee die Wahrheit enthält und doch etwas völlig Falsches wiedergibt?

Meine Wahrnehmung auf die Sinne zu richten, statt auf die Geschichte, war gewissermassen mein Versuch, die blinde Beobachtung der Schönheit zu überwinden. Um den Ort so zu beschreiben, wie mein Körper ihn wahrnahm, musste ich beides wahrnehmen. Anstatt von aussen nach innen zu schauen, musste ich mich, in die Welt, über die ich schrieb, hineinversetzen, wie Merleau-Ponty es nannte.

Jeder Kanton, den ich erkundete, hatte eine ausgeprägte Identität. Wenn Schwyz im eigenen Selbstverständnis die Urschweiz war, der Kanton, aus dem schliesslich auch Name und Fahne des Landes stammten, dann war Uri die Seele und die Kraft des Landes.

Auch wenn ich mich bemühte, die Klischees eines jeden Ortes auszublenden, entging mir nicht, wie man mit den Augen rollte, als ich die gepflegten Gärten in Schwyz erwähnte, einer Region, die als reich und konservativ bekannt ist, oder wie man mich belächelte, als ich über die dunklen Mauern von Uri sprach, einem Ort, der als so engstirnig gilt wie das Tal selbst. Nur über Unterwalden schwieg man seltsamerweise.

Ich versuchte, mich so gut es ging von diesen Vorurteilen zu befreien, um in die Landschaften selbst einzutauchen. Ich war neugierig, ob sich Unterschiede zwischen den benachbarten Gebieten herauskristallisieren, oder ob ihre Besonderheiten nur eine Frage meiner kulturell geprägten Vorstellungen sind.

Als ich die niedergeschriebenen Eindrücke der einzelnen Kantone betrachtete, war ich überrascht, wie unterschiedlich sie sich auf dem Blatt formten: Die blühende Schönheit von Schwyz steht in scharfem Kontrast zur Wildheit der zerklüfteten Urner Landschaft. Die Eigenheiten der einzelnen Kantone traten im Text zum Vorschein und schärften sich in gegenseitiger Abgrenzung.

Nur in Unterwalden verwischten die Grenzen schneller. Es war, als hätte das Land auch nach all den Jahren die 1340 vollzogene politische Teilung in die beiden Halbkantone Obwalden und Nidwalden nie richtig abgeschlossen.

Während die imposanten Urner Bergrücken mich selten vergessen liessen, wo ich mich befand, war es in Unterwalden schwerer, sich zurechtzufinden. Hier verliefen die Grenzen träge durch weite Täler und auf halbe Höhe, um dann wieder in ausgedehntes Grün hinabzusinken.

Wie ein schattenstörendes Objekt hielt es die klaren Konturen der anderen in der Schwebe.

Es ist nun mehr als zwei Jahre her, dass ich die 21 Wanderungen durch die Kantone gemacht habe. Während die Details eines jeden Ortes zwischen den Gitterlinien der Landkarte verblassen, bin ich mir immer noch nicht sicher, ob ich nun mehr oder weniger zur Schweiz gehöre.

Ich habe ein Protokoll erstellt, wo es keines gab. Ich habe mich in eine Erzählung hinein- und wieder herausgeschrieben.

Ich habe mir meinen eigenen Weg der Initiation gebahnt.

Ich habe geglaubt.

Ich bin den Grenzen gefolgt, habe sie auswendig gelernt, bin gelaufen, bis meine müden Beine von der Eroberung eines jeden Kantons schmerzten – und dennoch läuft mein Student*innenvisum in viereinhalb Monaten ab.

Der Gedanke, dass im Gründungsdokument dieses Landes die Pronomen durcheinandergeraten sind, ist für mich tröstlich. Im Raum zwischen „wir“ und „sie“ rutscht das Selbst immer wieder über die Grenzen des Anderen. Als ob ein gewisser Anteil Fremdheit Voraussetzung für eine angemessene Beziehung ist. Für das, was es bedeutet, dazuzugehören.

SCHWYZ

Auf einmal bin ich ganz klein in einem Land voller tiefer, tiefer Täler, als ob sich die Landschaft erhoben und mich verschluckt hätte. Der See liegt hinter mir und ich bin umhüllt von Bergen. Von beiden Seiten werde ich von grünen Wänden getragen, mit Bauernhöfen verstreut an den steilen Hängen. Ein Grün so durchdringend, dass es sich dem Auge verwehrt. Die Farbe schwebt und hebt sich vom Gras ab in Wellen von Wärme.

Vor diesem Moment, noch bevor ich meine Ohren spitze, wenn der Name des heimlichen Schwarms fällt, gibt es für mich den Kanton nicht. Ich setze einen Fuss in Schwyz und bin verloren. Ich überschreite eine unsichtbare Grenze und tauche in die Gegenwärtigkeit eines Ortes ein.

Von Basel, meiner Heimat am Rande der Schweiz, trete ich jede Woche die Reise ins Innere des Landes an. Jeden Samstag stehe ich im Morgengrauen auf, flechte mein Haar, reibe meine Haut mit Sonnencreme ein, schnüre die Senkel meiner Schuhe und steige in das erste Tram zum Bahnhof.

Woche für Woche, Zugfahrt für Zugfahrt, Weg für Weg, erscheint der Kanton vor meinen Augen.

Am Ufer des Sihlsees steigt eine kleine Rauchsäule von einem entfernten Strand auf. Es ist noch früher Morgen und das brennende Holz füllt die Luft mit einem Duft nach Zeder und Myrrhe. Die Schatten und Formen von Häusern am anderen Ufer reflektieren auf der Wasseroberfläche, ein Spiegel von Wasserfarben, während am anderen Ufer die Hügel unter grünen Decken in die Höhe wachsen.

Ein Traktor fährt einen Feldweg hoch zu einer Scheune aus dunklem Holz. Eine getigerte Katze liegt auf dem Asphalt und rollt sich in der Sonne auf die andere Seite.

Wiesen werden zu Wäldern, als der Pfad zum Fuss des angrenzenden Berges ansteigt. Meine Waden schmerzen schon bei den ersten Schritten des Tages. Mein Atem wird schneller. Mein Herz klopft.

Unter dem Schiff der Kathedrale schrumpfen die hölzernen Kirchenbänke neben Wänden aus grellweissem Stuck. Die Decke wölbt sich zu einer dunklen Kuppel mit Engelsfresken, die durch schwarze Gewitterwolken herabsteigen.

Der Altarraum ist voller Heiligen, wie in einer Hexengruft, in der jeder Feind zu Stein geworden ist. Die heilige Agatha steht mit abgetrennten Brüsten auf einer goldenen Platte. Zu ihren Füssen liegt ein Skelett in einer Glasvitrine, auf einen Ellbogen gestützt und die Finger geschmückt mit Juwelen.

Über den Kirchenbänken tragen vier steinerne Figuren eine Kanzel aus rosa und goldenem Marmor. Junge Männer mit gekrümmten Hälsen, ihre Rücken gebeugt unter dem Gewicht. An den Muskeln ihrer Arme kräuseln sich die Adern. Den gewölbten Fusssohlen, die direkt über meinem Kopf schweben, neide ich die Festigkeit jedes einzelnen Marmorzehs, der sich vor Leben biegt.

Schneewehen verschwinden in Felsspalten, bevor sie ins Donnern der Wasserfälle schmelzen. Im Licht der späten Nachmittagssonne leuchtet das Meeresgrün des unteren Felsens auf und verblasst wieder; die Farben wechseln wie in einem Kaleidoskop aus Jadeschatten.

Ich ersehne meine Reisen in den Kanton Schwyz wie eine Droge, ohne die ich unruhig werde. Ich studiere die Landkarte und mit jedem Entfalten entdecke ich neue Orte, an die meine Routen mich noch hinführen werden.

Ich erbitte Schwyz eher als dass ich es erobere. Jede Woche pilgere ich in das Zentrum des Landes und bitte darum, eingelassen zu werden.

Ein gezackter Horizont aus weisser Wildnis erhebt sich weit über einem See, dessen azurblauer Mantel den Fuss der Berge umhüllt.

Die Schneedecke zerbricht unter meinen Füssen. Ich höre das Krachen der Kristalle. Mein Fuss verschwindet in einer Mulde. Durch meine Wollsocken schmelzen die Eisflocken auf meiner Haut.

Die Glocken eines markanten Kirchturms läuten zur vollen Stunde und überdecken das Scheppern der Kuhglocken. An der Hauptstrasse gibt es einen Coop, eine Bäckerei, eine Post, ein Haus mit zugezogenen Spitzengardinen.

Hinter den hohen Feldern, auf denen ein Bauer Heu mäht, liegen die gepflegten Rasenflächen eines Golfplatzes. Darauf gleiten Carts über gepflasterte Wege und Männer schützen ihre Augen mit Visieren vor dem grellen Licht der schneebedeckten Berge. Gelbe Schilder mahnen die Wanderer, sich vor fliegenden Golfbällen in Acht zu nehmen.

Eine Wolke schiebt sich über die Sonne, es wird dunkler und die Sicht schärfer, und ich beobachte, wie sich die Landschaften wie ein Puzzle vor meinen Augen zusammenfügen.

Vom Gipfel der *Grossen Mythen* über die schwarz bewaldeten Hügel, die nach Einsiedeln führen, zu den Ufern des Sihlsees, wo ich vor Wochen auf den Felsen sass und dem Plätschern der Wellen lauschte, die sich mit dem Rauschen des Verkehrs und dem fernen Gesang der Alphörner vermischten.

An einem Wanderweg in der Nähe von Muotathal sehe ich den Namen *Hölloch* in ein Holzschild geschnitzt, das mit einem roten Pfeil in den Wald weist. Ein Schild in der Nähe erklärt, dass das *Hölloch* eine Höhle ist, dessen Gänge über 200 Kilometer lang, und fast eintausend Meter tief in das Gebirge hineinreichen. Unter dem Schild aus verzogenem Plastik hängt ein Foto von Besuchern, die unter ihren orangefarbenen Helmen lächeln, während sie bei Kerzenschein in der Höhle Wein und Raclette geniessen. Gegen eine beträchtliche Gebühr wird ein unvergessliches Erlebnis für „Outdoor-Liebhaber jeden Alters“ versprochen.

Die Höhle ist für dieses Jahr bereits geschlossen, aber für den Rest des Tages, an dem ich durch Hochtäler und entlang von Bergrücken mit Blick auf schneebedeckte Gipfel wandere, muss ich ständig an den enormen Innenraum unter meinen Füssen denken.

Es ist später Frühling und die Stadt steht in voller Blüte. Wolken ziehen über den hellen Himmel und die Luft ist erfüllt vom Duft zerzauster, weisser Blüten, die die Bäume schmücken. Kopfsteinpflasterstrassen führen entlang Herrenhäusern mit roten Geranien auf den Fensterbänken und Blick auf Gartenreihen mit Mangoldflügeln und Kohlblättern, die sich entfalten.

Im Zentrum der Stadt, im Schatten einer Kathedrale, befindet sich eine kleine Kapelle mit einer schweren Holztür. Darin liegt ein alter Mann in einem Sarg und wartet auf sein Begräbnis. Ein Bilderrahmen mit seinem lächelnden Foto steht daneben, doch die gepuderten Gesichtszüge sind kaum wieder zu erkennen. Die dünnen Augenlider und blassen Lippen wurden geschlossen und alle Gesichtsbehaarung von der puppenhaften Haut entfernt. Jetzt ist sie weich und glatt.

Ich gehe in tiefen, in die Erde gefurchten Rillen. Wände aus duftendem Laub erheben sich zu beiden Seiten schulterhoch, bis die Böschung in eine weitläufige Wiese mit weissen und gelben Wildblumen übergeht. Kühe weiden im hohen Gras, das sich unter den Kirschbäumen wiegt.

Es ist ein Feiertagswochenende und auf dem Weg wimmelt es von Touristen. Hinter jeder Biegung des Weges tauchen makellose Aussichten auf Alpen und Gletscherseen auf, eingebettet in einen geschliffenen Rahmen aus Wald und Himmel. Ich starre die Berge an. Ich mache Fotos, um ihre Realität zu dokumentieren, aber die fernen Gestalten erscheinen auf meinem Handy nur als Panorama aus dunstigen weissen Schatten.

Ich versuche dem Wind in den Bäumen zu lauschen, um das Gemurmel der Gespräche vor und hinter mir zu überhören. Ich spüre das Gewicht meiner Wanderschuhe, wenn sie über die verhärteten Schneeflecken schrammen.

Stunden vergehen. Nachdem ich ein paar Mal falsch abgebogen bin, sind die Touristen verschwunden. Ich merke, dass ich allein bin, auf der falschen Seite des Berges und der schnellste Weg führt gerade hinunter ins Tal. Ich lasse mich von der Schwerkraft tragen, verlasse den Pfad und hüpfe durch das Gras im Zickzack den Hang hinunter zu einem See, der die Farbe des Himmels hat.

URI

Am Anfang nähere ich mich Uri zentimeterweise. Ich habe keine Eile, die neugewonnene Vertrautheit mit Schwyz zu verlassen, mit seinen sanften Weiden und blühenden Bäumen, wo ich einst an einer Herde blökender Ziegen vorbeiging, die statt Glocken bimmelnde Windspiele um den Hals trugen.

Das Wappen von Uri, oft auf einen Felsblock entlang einer Strasse oder eines abgelegenen Weges gemalt, ist ein wilder Stier vor einem knallgelben Hintergrund. Man erkennt das Tier an den zusammengekniffenen Augen, der herausgestreckten Zunge und dem schweren Ring, der an seiner Nase hängt.

Ich schiebe die Reise auf, ich zögere, aber das Eintauchen in einen Kanton ist nicht abgeschlossen, ohne das Eintauchen in den anderen. Wie die Ringe eines Labyrinths schliessen sich und umschliessen dich die Kreise immer mehr, bis man im Zentrum ankommt.

Auf einem Grabstein ohne Namen ragt ein bärtiger Mann mit dichtem, windzerzaustem Haar aus dem Felsen und hebt sein gemeisseltes Gesicht hoch zu den Bergen.

Als ich in *Erstfeld* ankomme, versinkt die Sonne gerade hinter den dunklen Wänden des Tals. Ich suche die nächste Zugverbindung nach Basel. Am Kiosk kaufe ich einen Kaffee und frage die Frau hinter dem Schalter, wo die Altstadt ist. Sie lächelt ein wenig amüsiert: „Das ist sie."

Ich trete aus dem Bahnhof auf eine leere Strasse, auf der ich von jedem Fremden, der vorbeigeht, beobachtet werde. Ich laufe schneller, um den Blicken zu entgehen, vorbei an Fenstern mit gehäkelten Vorhängen und Plastikzwergen mit roten Mützen. Aber noch bevor ich meinen Kaffee ausgetrunken habe, bin ich am Ende der Stadt und laufe entlang einer Autostrasse ins Nirgendwo.

„Danke und auf Wiedersehen", steht auf einem gelben Schild.

Der Gipfel eines Berges erhebt sich, verschwindet und taucht dann wieder aus dem Nebelmeer auf. Wie eine Gestalt, die den ganzen Raum einnimmt, ist ihre Form selbst dann spürbar, wenn sie verhüllt ist.

Von beiden Seiten eines Bergrückens schwappen weisse Schwaden auf den Weg und bilden einen dreieckigen Korridor, durch den drei Wanderer schreiten. Wenig später werden sie vom Grau verschluckt. Ich höre nur noch ihre körperlosen Stimmen.

Dem Fluss folgend wie ein stählerner Schatten, ziehen sich Eisenbahnschienen durch den Talboden. Reihen mattroter Waggons mit stumpfen, kantigen Gesichtern stehen regungslos auf den Gleisen vor der Schwelle des Gotthardtunnels.

Der Weg folgt nicht der Oberfläche der Landschaft. Er führt mitten durch die zerfurchte Erde, sodass ich über Steine und Wurzeln trete, die aus dem Boden ragen. Wasserfälle stürzen über den Wanderweg. Der Weg führt nicht um die Kuhweiden herum, sondern mitten hindurch. Ich kann mich nicht an die Unermesslichkeit dieser schweren, braunen Körper in meiner Nähe gewöhnen, an die dicken, hervorstehenden Knochen ihrer Hinterteile und ihre kurzen, scharfen Hörner, während sie träge zusehen, wie ich auf Zehenspitzen vorbeischleiche.

Dicke Schneeplatten liegen zerbrochen vor mir und schmelzen. Zwischen ihren zackigen Rändern fliesst ein Bach unter den Wölbungen des restlichen Schnees hindurch.

In einer blinden Kurve neigt sich der Bus gegen eine Klippe, und das dreistimmige Horn ertönt wie eine Mischung aus sterbendem Alphorn und langsamem Krankenwagen. Noch eine Kurve und die Scheibe berührt eine Felswand. Raunen und nervöses Lachen der Passagiere, als der Bus sein Gleichgewicht zurückfindet und in einem schwarzen Loch, das in die Bergwand gesprengt wurde, verschwindet. Der Tunnel öffnet sich wieder über einer Schlucht mit sprudelndem Wasser, unterbrochen von gigantischen Felsblöcken, die sich gegen den Fluss des Wassers stemmen.

Das steinerne Fundament eines Chalets ist mit einem Hang so verschmolzen, dass sich die grüne Erdschicht wie eine Decke über das Haus legt.

Nebel hängt zwischen Felsspalten. Die kohlefarbenen Klüfte reichen zum limettenfarbenen Gras hinab, die gegen das dunkle Grau hell fluoreszieren.

Ich durchschreite eine Ebene mit rauchig-weissem Stein. Der helle Boden ist gesprenkelt mit dunklem Moos. In der harten Oberfläche gibt es grosse Vertiefungen, als ob jemand seine Fingerabdrücke in Ton hinterlassen hat. Zwischen den Rissen wachsen Grasbüschel aus feuchtem Seetang-farbenem Boden. Die Luft riecht stark nach Erde.

Ich kraxle über einen Felssturz mit Findlingen und zerbrochenem Schiefer und spüre förmlich das Poltern und Krachen der Steine, wenn ich anhalte.

Eines Abends, bevor ich Uri verlasse, liege ich im Bett und drücke ein Kissen gegen meine Brust. Seit Tagen ist da ein dumpfes, schmerzendes Pochen. Als ich das Licht lösche, höre ich schon den Wecker klingeln. Ich ziehe die Decke näher an mich ran und meine Beine werden schwer, als ich die Reise des nächsten Tages in meinen Gedanken durchgehe.

Der Wetterbericht warnt vor Gewittern.

Eine kleine, braune Schlange taucht auf dem Weg auf. Sie züngelt und schlüpft davon.

Ich setze mich in meinem Bett auf und ziehe Jeans, einen Sport-BH, ein Tanktop und einen Kapuzenpullover an. Ich löffle Kaffee in den Trichter auf dem Herd. Ich fülle meine Wasserflasche. Ich staple Brot- und Käsescheiben übereinander und versorge sie in einen Plastiksack. Ich streiche Sonnencreme wie Kriegsbemalung auf mein Gesicht. Zwischen zwei Schlucken Kaffee flechte ich meine Haare, steige in die Schuhe und trete aus der Tür. Mein Körper sträubt sich gegen die harten Tritte auf Asphalt, während ich renne und gerade noch zwischen den sich schliessenden Tramtüren hindurch schlüpfe.

Eine Schlucht öffnet sich zwischen zwei Bergen und heraus tritt mit Wucht ein Fluss. Das grüngraue Wasser wirbelt in weissen Stromschnellen vorwärts.

Hoch oben am bewaldeten Berghang sehe ich eine Kette von Wasserfällen, nicht als langsam an Kraft gewinnende Rinnsale, sondern als ausgewachsene Flüsse, die sich inmitten von Nebelschwaden von den Klippen stürzen.

Ich halte meinen Atem an beim Geruch von Abgasen und dem Gestank von Teer während ich dem Weg entlang der Bahngleise folge. Er führt mich gegen die Fahrtrichtung der Autos, die weit unten in den Gotthardtunnel kriechen. Ich kann den nahen Fluss und die ausdauernden Zikaden unter dem Dröhnen der Autos kaum hören, und doch empfinde ich die Durchgangsstrasse nicht als Bruch in der Landschaft, sondern vielmehr als bizarren Auswuchs einer rohen Kraft dieses Ortes.

Der Himmel verdunkelt sich, während die Sonne hinter aschfahlen Wolken verschwindet. Als wäre ein Filter über die Landschaft gelegt worden, wird das sanfte Grün tiefer und heller. Die Textur des zerklüfteten Erdrands tritt sichtbar hervor – ein in zwei Teile gerissener Teppich, durch den das blasse Wasser hindurchfliessen kann.

An einer Seilbahnstation, durch eine dünne Holztür und die Treppe hinauf, wird die kleine weisse Toilette von Sonnenlicht durchflutet, und das Fenster ist gekippt, damit die kühle Morgenluft eindringen kann. Ein frisches Handtuch hängt neben dem Waschbecken und eine neue Seife steht bereit.

Graue Steinpyramiden erheben sich vor einem blauen Himmel, während Nebel wie Weihrauch über der Ebene aufsteigt.

In einer Berghütte steht ein Holzregal an einer Felswand, das vom Boden bis zur Decke mit Gummi-Cloqs vollgestopft ist. Jedes Paar ist sorgfältig so angeordnet, dass der Absatz des einen in die Spitze des anderen passt. Wie in einer Schachtel mit Farbstiften sind die Hausschuhe nach Farben geordnet. Je ein Regal für Weiss, Mintgrün, Rosa, Orange und drei Blautöne.

Ich gehe an dem Schuhregal vorbei in ein leeres Esszimmer, rustikale Kronleuchter hängen über langen Tischen, an denen Stühle mit dicken, geschnitzten Lehnen stehen. An den hölzernen Wänden hängen verblasste Gemälde mit Alpenmotiven neben spitzengerahmten Fenstern, die fast die gleiche Aussicht freigeben.

Ich laufe in eine Wand aus Nebel, schlüpfe mit meinen Händen in die Ärmel und ziehe meine Kapuze hoch. Ein kalter Wind weht über den nackten Boden.

Es war eine vierstündige Fahrt von Basel, nach einer Nacht mit wenig Schlaf, aber ich bin hellwach, als der Bus den Berg hinauffährt. Die enge, kurvenreiche Strasse steigt höher und höher an, und als ich schon denke, wir hätten den Gipfel erreicht, briecht die Sonne durch und der Bus klettert noch höher, bis ich unter mir Vögel in der Luft kreisen sehe und über mir gezackte Felsen aus dem wolkenverhangenen Himmel ragen.

Am Ausgangspunkt des Weges beklagt ein Wanderer, dass die beeindruckende Aussicht nun vom Nebel verdeckt wird. Ich bin jedoch fast erleichtert nichts zu sehen, ständig in Sorge, der Schönheit unter mir nicht würdig zu sein.

Als ich den Boden der abfallenden Mulde erreiche, die von den umliegenden Bergen geformt wurde, spüre ich den Schmerz in meinen Knien. Die Erleichterung über die flache Schotterpiste ist nur von kurzer Dauer, denn diese führt zu einem weiteren Abstieg um zweitausend Meter. Meine Knie zittern jedes Mal, wenn meine Füsse den Boden berühren, und die Schärfe des Schmerzes lässt mich alle paar Meter anhalten.

Ich versuche, seitwärts zu gehen; ich versuche, neben dem Weg zu gehen, um meine Schritte auf Grashügeln abzufedern, ich versuche, zu gehen, ohne meine Beine zu beugen, aber nichts kann den Schmerz in meinen Knie lindern.

Als ich am späten Abend wieder in Basel aussteige, humple ich gebückt aus dem Zug, betrübt über meine Niederlage.

An der Hauptstrasse hängen an zwei Ketten die grossen Vorderpfoten eines Bären in einem Schaufenster. An der Unterseite der dicken Krallen sind noch Fellbüschel zu sehen, aber die runzlige Haut ist vom Alter grau geworden. Ein Schild bestätigt, dass es sich um die Überreste des letzten Bären handelt, der in diesem Tal erlegt wurde.

Die Luft ist weiss und unbewegt. Der Boden ist mit feuchtem Laub bedeckt, braun und gelb mit Flecken von sterbendem Grün. Der Weg öffnet sich zu einer Landzunge, die in die Leere des Nebels reicht, wo die Baumkronen wie Schatten auftauchen. Für einen Moment lichtet sich der Schleier und eine Felswand, riesig und erschreckend nah, erscheint an meiner Seite.

Ich höre Schritte hinter mir. Ich drehe mich um und sehe den ersten Wanderer, dem ich heute begegnet bin, einen blassen Mann in den Dreissigern, der eine armeegrüne Jacke trägt. Er hat einen zotteligen Bart und schwarzes Haar zu einer Topf-Frisur geschnitten. Er weicht meinem Blick aus und sagt nichts, als er vorbeigeht. Ich beschleunige den Schritt, während ich nach dem Taschenmesser in meinem Mantel taste. Für den Rest des Weges gehe ich unerbittlich durch den nebligen Wald mit seinen knochendünnen Bäumen. Bei jeder Abzweigung werfe ich einen Blick zurück, aber der Weg verschwindet jedesmal im Nebel. Ich beeile mich weiterzugehen, durch Wolkenfetzen hindurch, die über den Weg schweben.

Die Stämme der Bäume sind mit Moos überwachsen und verzweigen sich in fingerartige Wurzeln, die sich in den Boden graben.

In der warmen Atmosphäre einer Kapelle flackert eine lange Kerze neben einem kleinen Sarg. Das tropfende Wachs ist mit bunten Figuren von Kindern verziert, jedes hält die Hand des anderen und sie bilden einen Ring um die flackernde Flamme. An der Wand darüber hängt Jesus mit einem goldenen Lendenschurz am Kreuz, daneben Figuren von trauernden Heiligen und grimmigen Engeln, die über die Toten wachen.

Als ich mich dem offenen Sarg nähere, stelle ich mir bereits den kindlichen Leichnam vor, den mir die regenbogenfarbene Kerze angekündigt hat. Mein Herz klopft in meiner Brust. Ich neige mein Gesicht nach vorne und gehe einen Schritt näher, obwohl mich mein Körper zurückhält. Das Innere des Sarges rückt in meinen Blick, leer und wartend.

Oberhalb des Weges hängt an einem Baum ein riesiges Windspiel, jedes Rohr so gross wie ein kleiner Baseballschläger. Die metallenen Röhren klingen längst nicht mehr, sondern scheppern nur noch wie die Werkzeuge eines unaufgeräumten Werkzeugkastens.

UNTERWALDEN

An einem Samstagmorgen am Ufer des Vierwaldstättersees werden vor der örtlichen Drogerie Bettflaschen in gestrickten Jäckchen verkauft. Der Nebel umhüllt die Stadt wie ein Morgenmantel und hängt tief über dem Wasser, während die Wellen sanft über die Kieselsteine an der leeren Uferpromenade schwappen.

In der Bäckerei versammeln sich die Leute um lange Holztische unter dem warmen Licht einer Lampe vor einer mit Blumen bedruckten Tapete. An der Wand hängen Schwarzweissfotos von Frauen, die kunstvoll verzierte Torten bestaunen.

Ich bin zum ersten Mal in Nidwalden und mir fällt sofort das Fehlen von Kantonsfahnen auf. Was ich sehe, als ich durch die Stadt gehe, ist ein kleines rotes Tuch, das von einem Blumentopf herunterweht.

In den folgenden Wochen achte ich auf die Grenze zwischen Nidwalden und Obwalden, doch es ist schwierig, den einen Kanton zu erkunden, ohne in den anderen zu stolpern.

Selbst der markante Gebirgszug zwischen den beiden Tälern ist keine zuverlässige Schranke. Ich steige in Obwalden in eine Seilbahn, schwebe auf halbe Höhe eines Berges hinauf und steige in Nidwalden aus, wo sich die scharfen Kanten des schneebedeckten Gipfels gegen einen weissen Himmel abheben.

Es ist früher Abend, und die bewaldeten Hänge einer Schlucht schimmern in Purpur- und Goldtönen. Weit unten in den Bäumen versteckt sich ein Kloster. Vom Flussbett aus geht ein Mönch den Weg entlang und unterhält sich mit einem anderen Mann. Sein dunkles Gewand wiegt sich im langsamen Rhythmus seiner Bewegungen.

Auf der Veranda eines Luxushotels mit Blick auf die Schlucht stehen die Gäste fröstelnd und rauchend und werfen gelegentlich einen Blick auf das Alpenbild, eingerahmt von den fruchtbaren Wänden des Tals.

Früh morgens sitze ich im Zug nach Stans neben einer älteren Frau in einem knallroten Hosenanzug. Immer wieder beugt sie sich nach vorne und spricht mit ihrer schwerhörigen Begleiterin, die ihre Freundin mit einem angestrengten, aber geduldigen Lächeln immer wieder bitten muss, ihre Aussage zu wiederholen. Bald gibt die alte Frau das Gespräch auf und wendet sich mir zu. Als sie merkt, dass ich kein Schweizerdeutsch spreche, lässt sie sich nicht beirren. Ihre dichten Falten gehen in ein Grinsen über, ich sähe mit meinen zwei Zöpfen aus wie Gretel aus dem Märchen. Ich bin überrascht, dass sie in mir nicht Heidi sieht, mit der ich viel öfter verglichen werde.

Ich gehe durch Vorhänge aus gelben Blättern.

Der grüne Teppich in der Senke ist so breit, dass ich fast vergesse, dass ich mich in einem Tal befinde. Vom Bahnhof aus entrollen sich vor mir glatte, ebene Strassen in der Sonne. Ich gehe vorbei an einer Frau, die mir von der Veranda ihres gelben Hauses zulächelt, vorbei an einem alten Mann, der sich über die verworrenen Reben seines Gartens beugt. Er blickt auf und grüsst ein Mädchen, das ihm von ihrem aus Fahrrad zuwinkt.

Ich habe das schleichende Gefühl, auf einem Filmset zu stehen, als eine Frau anhält und fragt, ob ich eine Wegbeschreibung brauche. Ich finde ihre detaillierten Angaben absolut einleuchtend. Die Luft ist kühl und duftet vertraut nach frisch gemähtem Heu und dem brennenden Holz eines nahen Feuers.

Entblätterte Äste bilden einen Bogen über dem Weg. Letzte gelbe Fetzen hängen zwischen den Bäumen wie Konfetti in der Luft. Auf dem Boden, unter einer Schicht bernstein- und kupferfarbener Blätter, hat sich der Teppich tiefschwarz verfärbt.

Ich spüre, wie die kahlen Hügel sanft dahinrollen, ihre wollig-grünen Hänge so gross und nah, als würden schlafende Kreaturen neben mir atmen.

Der Bus nach Oberrickenbach ist weniger ein Bus, als ein kleiner Lieferwagen, der an der Haltestelle wartet. Er ist leer bis auf den bärtigen Fahrer, der seine Hände mustert, während er den beschwingten Klängen eines Akkordeons im Radio lauscht. Als er den Motor startet, schaut er mich durch den Rückspiegel an und sagt, die Seilbahn in Oberrickenbach sei geschlossen. Dann dreht er die Musik auf und schon bald fahren wir im Zickzack den Berg hinauf.

Als wir das Dorf erreichen, jodelt es aus dem Radio. Der Wagen wird von einer Schafherde angehalten, die die Strasse überquert, während in der Ferne ein Traktor vor sich hin rumpelt. Durch das Fenster sehe ich einen Bauern, der einen Baumstamm nach dem anderen einen steilen Abhang hinunterrollt.

Nebel umhüllt silberne, eisige Felder, in denen jeder Halm, jedes Blatt und jede Blüte kristallweiss umrandet ist.

Als würde ich aus dem Grau in eine Welt der Farben auftauchen, trete ich aus dem nebligen Wald heraus. Ich sehe, wie der Nebel schnell den Berghang hinunterspült, und sich wieder zurückzieht wie eine Flut, die in der aufgehenden Sonne glänzt. Innerhalb von Sekunden offenbart sich um mich herum ein Alpenpanorama. Ich stehe am Fuss hoher Wände und aufragender Zinnen, kolossaler Gestalten, die noch vor wenigen Augenblicken nichts weiter als blasse Schatten im Nebel gewesen waren.

Unmittelbar unter der Bergkette erhebt sich ein Erdwall, und von der anderen Seite, die wie aus einer unsichtbaren Leere auftaucht, steigen Wolkenwellen auf und rollen über den Kamm. Ich folge der Spur der Wand entlang und stelle fest, dass ich auf die Mauer eines Staudamms blicke, der in eine Bergkuppe gemeisselt ist. Die Wolken über dem dunklen Wasser, noch unerreicht von der Sonne, schlagen Purzelbäume.

Auf dem verschneiten Parkplatz spielt Popmusik aus den Lautsprechern. Die Hits verfolgen mich durch die elektrischen Türen zum Ticketschalter, zu den Toiletten und in die lange, schummrige Halle mit rosa Techno-Lichtern, die zu den langsam zirkulierenden Gondeln führt.

Vorsichtig trete ich in den kleinen, schwebenden Raum. Das goldene Logo des Titlis ist quer über die Rückseite des schwarzen Teppichsitzes gedruckt, darunter die Umrisse eines wellenförmigen Gipfels. Ich bin immer noch allein, als sich die Türen schliessen. Die Gondel gleitet vorwärts und erhebt sich lautlos in die Luft. Die Skisaison ist noch nicht eröffnet, und mindestens zwanzig leere Gondeln passieren, jede mit einer Flagge eines anderen Landes oder Kantons versehen.

An einem stillen Morgen lässt ein allein stehender Baum totes Laub fallen. Von seinen Ästen tropft es unablässig auf den Weg, wie in einem Moment der Erleichterung, lange nachdem der Wind sich verabschiedet hat.

Hinter einem Gipfel verschwindet der Tag in einer blauen Glut und hüllt ihn in einen leuchtenden Schein. Schneeflocken wehen von der Spitze, sie kräuseln sich, lösen sich auf und vergehen.

Ich atme ein, als wäre es das erste Mal. Mein Atem füllt meine Lungen.

Die Sonne ist ein weisser Ball, der sich im schwarzen Marmor eines Sees spiegelt. Eisplatten reichen bis zur Mitte des Sees, dessen Tiefe unter der Reflexion der Berge verborgen ist. Jede Falte, jede Kräuselung des umliegenden Gesteins ist mit Schnee überzogen. Das anhaltende Dröhnen einer Maschine, die den blassen Dampf erzeugt, verfolgt mich auf dem Weg.

Es dauert lange, bis die Gondelstation und die verstreuten Hütten hinter den Stracciatella-farbenen Hügeln verschwinden und ich nur noch das Knirschen meiner Schritte auf dem Boden und das Rascheln der gepolsterten Kapuze meiner Jacke höre.

Am Horizont der zerklüfteten Alpen schlängeln sich die Pfade entlang seidener Dünen aus weissem Pulver. Meine Augen schmerzen von der Helligkeit des Bodens, während ich schwerfälligen Tritts auf meine Schneeschuhe blicke. Bei jedem Kontakt fliegen Flocken auf und glitzern in der Luft.

Ein Schwarm weisser Vögel gleitet über ein Dorf. Über metallenen Lagerhallen, den Bahnhof, die Traktoren, die übereinander gestapelten Wohnungen, die offenen Türen der Kathedrale, deren bodenlange Vorhänge zur Seite gezogen sind, um den Wind durchzulassen.

Die Vögel sind eine langsame, stille Welle von Körpern, die sich auf und ab bewegen, bevor sie sich in zwei Sphären auflösen. Die Form schwankt und löst sich in der grauen Luft auf, während die ersten Regentropfen fallen.

Sich in die Schweiz einschreiben

Was macht die Schweizer*in aus und wie wird frau zu einer solchen? Dieser Frage geht Shelby Stuart in ihrem Text wortwörtlich nach. Sie erwandert sich gleichsam die Schweizer Staatsbürgerschaft, indem sie die drei sogenannten Waldstätten Uri, Schwyz und Unterwalden durchstreift, betrachtet, erlebt und beschreibt. Zwar hat sie schweizerische Vorfahren, dazwischen liegt aber eine expatriierte Generation. Deshalb erhält sie zunächst nur ein Studentinnenvisum, das immer wieder verlängert werden muss. Das Verfahren, um das sogenannte Bürger*innenrecht zu erhalten, ist langsam und aufwändig. Shelby beginnt unterdessen schon mal damit, sich zu integrieren. Im Gesetz wird diese wichtige Voraussetzung für die Staatsbürger*innenschaft genau beschrieben. Die politische Haltung der Verfasser schimmert dabei ziemlich direkt durch; es ist klar, gegen wen sich die Beschreibung richtet: „Eine erfolgreiche Integration zeigt sich insbesondere: (a.) im Beachten der öffentlichen Sicherheit und Ordnung; (b.) in der Respektierung der Werte der Bundesverfassung; (c.) in der Fähigkeit, sich im Alltag in Wort und Schrift in einer Landessprache zu verständigen; (d.) in der Teilnahme am Wirtschaftsleben oder am Erwerb von Bildung ... ."[1] Von einer Integration in die Landschaft und der persönlichen Einschreibung in die Geschichte ist natürlich keine Rede. Wie eine solche ablaufen könnte, zeigt indes Shelby Stuart sehr schön und überzeugend in ihrem Text. Sie setzt sich der alpinen Innerschweiz aus und wird dadurch tatsächlich, und nicht bloss juristisch Teil des Landes; und sie schreibt sich darin ein.

---

[1] Art. 12 BüG.

„Wenn die Grenzen feststehen, bekommen wir einen Platz. Wir gehören dazu“ (S. 66), notiert sie, wandert den Grenzen der sogenannten Urkantone entlang, erkundet, ob sie sich auch in der Landschaft zeigen und ob Unterschiede in der Stimmung der einzelnen Kantone auszumachen sind, in deren Ausgestaltung. Dabei gleicht sie auch immer wieder Klischee, Vorstellung und Gegenwart miteinander ab.
Die drei Waldstätten, die für Shelby Stuarts Text titelgebenden Kantone Schwyz, Uri und Unterwalden, werden oft mit der Gründung der Schweiz im Jahre 1291 in Verbindung gebracht. Heute bestehen Zweifel an der historischen Korrektheit dieser Datierung wie auch überhaupt am Gründungmythos. Möglicherweise wurde das Datum erst im Nachhinein so genau festgelegt, etwa um die 600-Jahrfeier der sogenannten Eidgenossenschaft zu untermauern. Die Gründung des Staates fand jedenfalls erst sehr viel später statt. Relativ gewiss ist indes, dass sich die Bewohner*innen der Innerschweiz um 1300 eher der Viehzucht widmeten, während im Mittelland Getreide angepflanzt wurde. Entsprechend waren alle auf Handel angewiesen. Zudem waren die Innerschweizer als Wehrmänner geschätzt und wurden von den städtischen Gebieten bisweilen zur Verteidigung engagiert.[2] In diesem Austausch von Kräften und Gütern, von Schutz, Diensten und Absatzmärkten liegt wohl die Motivation zum Bündnis, aus dem dereinst die Schweiz entstehen sollte. Vielleicht war dessen Grundlage ja schlicht der Gedanke, einander gegenseitig zu unterstützen. Mit der Landschaft hat das insofern zu tun, als sich die gebirgigen Lagen weder zur Gründung grösserer Städte noch für grossflächige Landwirtschaft eignen. Auch liessen sich die alpinen Streusiedlungen weniger gut kontrollieren und steuern

[2] Vgl. Thomas Maissen, Geschichte der Schweiz. Stuttgart 2015, S. 30 f.

als städtische Strukturen. Indem sich also unterschiedliche Gebiete mit ihren Stärken und Schwächen (und keinesfalls nur Gleiche mit Gleichen) zusammentaten, entstand mit der Zeit eine Nation.

Shelby Stuart macht auch diese geografische Austauschbewegung mit, die mit der Entstehung der Schweiz als Staat verbunden ist, wenn sie jeweils am Wochenende von Basel aus in die sogenannten Urkantone reist, um diese zu bewandern und ihre Eindrücke niederzuschreiben. Sie fährt dabei mit der Bahn von der Grenzstadt am Dreiländereck durch das Ackerbau- und Industriegebiet im Mittelland, steigt manchmal vielleicht in Luzern, der vierten und städtischsten Waldstätte um und wagt sich dann in die Alpentäler und Berge hoch, wo auch heute noch die Viehzucht vorherrscht. Dabei stellt sich ihr nicht nur die Frage, wie man Schweizerin wird, sondern auch diejenige, was das nun genau eigentlich ist, die Schweiz.

"Als ob ein gewisser Anteil Fremdheit Voraussetzung für eine angemessene Beziehung ist. Für das, was es bedeutet, dazuzugehören" (S. 78), so scheint es ihr. Und sie trifft damit vielleicht auch aus historischer Sicht ins Schwarze. Die Vielfalt, das Zusammenleben unterschiedlichster Menschen in einer sehr abwechslungsreichen Landschaft ist es, was – nebst der Landschaft selbst – die Schweiz ausmacht. Und insofern sollte es allen, die das wollen, möglich sein und möglich gemacht werden, sich zum Beispiel durch intensives Wandern darin einzuschreiben.

Christian de Simoni

Shelby Stuart (*1982/BS) is a transdisciplinary artist and author whose writing practice focuses on the senses as the starting point for the stories she chooses to tell. Her work spans from lyric essays and autoethnographic novels to texts rooted in a performative practice. In 2021, Shelby Stuart completed her M.A. in Transdisciplinary Studies at Zürich University of the Arts (ZHdK). More: shelbylstuart.com

Beatrice Minger (*1980) ist Autorin und Regisseurin und lebt in Zürich. Sie studierte Filmwissenschaft, Germanistik und Geschichte und übersetzt regelmässig Texte im Bereich Kunst und Kultur ins Deutsche.

Christian de Simoni liest und schreibt eigene und fremde Texte in Bern. Er ist Mitglied des Kollektivs *Hybrido Unreim.* Zuletzt erschien: *Das Rigilied. Herkunft und Bedeutung* (2017), *B586D431 H376F845E56. Kryptolyrik* (2017), *wandern/schreiben* (2023). Mehr: christiandesimoni.ch

edition taberna kritika
Neuerscheinungen 2022/23

André Vladimir Heiz
Kein Thema
ISBN 978-3-905846-72-0

Anina Mirjam Schärer
Im ausgeschriebenen Haus
ISBN 978-3-905846-71-3

Hartmut Abendschein
Concrete Strategies
ISBN 978-3-905846-70-6

Christian de Simoni
wandern/schreiben
ISBN 978-3-905846-69-4

Bojan Savić Ostojić
Punkt
ISBN 978-3-905846-68-3

Hannes Bajohr
Renga Anger
ISBN 978-3-905846-67-6

Daniele Pantano
HIMMEL-BIMMEL-BAM-BAM
ISBN 978-3-905846-66-9

edition taberna kritika
Gutenbergstrasse 47
CH - 3011 Bern
Tel.: +41 (0) 77 425 2 180
info@etkbooks.com | http://www.etkbooks.com